CARING ENOUGH TO HEAR

and Be Heard

David Augsburger

HERALD PRESS
Scottdale, Pennsylvania
Kitchener, Ontario

153.6
AUC

Other good reading:
Caring Enough to Confront by David
    Augsburger
*Caring Enough to Forgive/Caring Enough to
    Not Forgive* by David Augsburger

The foreign language publishing of all Regal books is under the direction of Gospel Literature International GLINT. GLINT provides financial and technical help for the adaptation, translation and publishing of books for millions of people worldwide. For information regarding translation, contact: GLINT, P.O. Box 6688, Ventura, California 93006.

Scripture quotations in this publication are, for the most part, the author's paraphrase. The rest are from the *Revised Standard Version* of the Bible, copyright 1946 and 1952 by the Division of Christian Education of the NCCC, U.S.A., and used by permission.

Herald Press edition published at Scottdale, PA 15683

  Released simultaneously in Canada by
  Herald Press, Kitchener, Ont. N2G 4M5

Library of Congress Catalog Card Number: 82-81000
International Standard Book Number: 0-8361-3307-2
Printed in the United States of America
83 84 85 86 87 88 10 9 8 7 6 5 4 3 2

HERALD PRESS
Scottdale, Pennsylvania
Kitchener, Ontario

Deep within our humanness is a profound need to be heard and understood—not in part but as a whole.

Discover how to meet this need—in yourself and in others.

CARING ENOUGH TO HEAR AND BE HEARD

Introduction

My side of the argument is clear. Your side is occasionally confused.

My side of the issue is logical. Your side is sometimes irrational.

My side of the hassle is justified. Your side is frequently unwarranted.

My side of the conflict is crucial. Your side is often unnecessary.

My side of the conversation makes sense to me, it is my experience of a vivid slice of human existence. But your side is "the other side." I have not experienced it; I do not understand it.

"Experiencing the other side" is, in Martin Buber's words, "the heart of dialogue." Feeling any experience from the side of the other person as well as from one's own side can make the experience twice as rich. Seeing any event through the other's eyes in addition to one's own makes the scene truly three dimensional.

The art of dialogue is openness to the other side, a willingness to enter the other's turf and to explore it until it is familiar territory. The heart of dialogue is coming to value a place near the center, on the boundary, where the other person's perspective is valued alongside my own. At this point of meeting, I become as concerned for the clarity of the other's stance as for my own; as willing to contribute an argumentative point to the other side as to assert one on my own; as committed to supporting the other's right to be at his or her position as I am to claim my own. Both sides are a gift, a gift to each other in our building responsive human community, a gift of God who calls us to create a community of grace.

Caring Enough to Hear and Be Heard is third in the series of caring books, following *Caring Enough to Confront* and *Caring Enough to Forgive/Caring Enough to Not Forgive*. The purpose of this volume is to evoke new understandings of the power of equal listening, attending, hearing, leveling, risking and caring in relationships, and to invite new experiments and experiences of being with others in equal communication and equal regard.

The richest moments and the most significant learnings about living in equal regard have come from the relationship with my life partner, Nancy, who has been a co-traveler with me from the pain of vertical communication to the intimacy of shared dialogue. The personal references throughout the book reflect her equal contribution to the discoveries reported here.

I am grateful also to great thinkers, teachers, colleagues who have invited me to learn the art of communication. The apostles Paul and John on the nature of love, Sören Kierkegaard and Martin Buber on the nature of dialogue, Paul Tillich and Gene Outka on justice and equal regard, Frank Kimper and Robert Meye for modeling dialogue, and to my colleagues at the Associated Mennonite Biblical Seminaries for our joint venture of working out equal regard in Christian community.

And to you, as we co-explore the art of communication in these pages.

David Augsburger
Goshen, Indiana.
Autumn, 1981

No one can develop freely in this world and find a full life without feeling understood by at least one person. No one comes to know himself through introspection, or in the solitude of his personal diary. Rather it is in dialogue, in his meeting with other persons.
Paul Tournier[1]

Human communication revolves chiefly around two kinds of speech: silent speech (listening) and overt speech (talking). Silent speech is the necessary preliminary to overt speech, and the quality of overt speech cannot be better than the quality of silent speech from which it springs. Overt speech can be understood only through the medium of the silent speech from which it emerges. One's expressive powers can never exceed his silent powers.
Paul W. Keller, Charles T. Brown[2]

1 ■ Listening

"Tell me again, I want to hear you."

"Tell me your name," I invite, hunkering down in front of the little boy. I had just shaken hands with the mother in the waiting room of the counseling center. They had come for their first appointment because, the note from our receptionist explained, "the boy was a kindergarten dropout."

The little boy looked at me emptily, glanced to his mother for help, then back to me.

"What is your name?" I repeated gently.

He inhaled, opened his mouth to speak . . .

"Johnny," the mother said, cutting in as if on cue.

"How old are you?" I asked.

Johnny looked first to his mother then again to me. Gathering courage he opened his mouth.

"Five," the mother said, with accurate timing.

I looked at her more closely, almost expecting to see an uncut umbilical cord still connecting the two.

"Johnny is almost six. I'm so worried because next year he's supposed to start first grade . . ."

(Johnny's eyes brighten.)

". . . and he'll go away on the big yellow bus . . ."

(Johnny's a big big boy who will be going to school.)

". . . and he'll be far away from Mommie and have to stay there all day and if he cries Mommie won't be there to help."

(Johnny's still a little boy who can't get along without Mommie.)

". . . so I'm afraid of school starting this fall."

(Or is it, as she inadvertently reveals, Mother who can't get along without Johnny?)

Johnny is a boy who is not being heard. Can I help his mother hear him?

Mrs. Jones is a mother who is not being heard. Her husband is distant, over-involved in his business, with little time for his wife or his son. They have grown almost as one in an unhealthy symbiosis. They have all forgotten—if they ever knew—how to listen, how to truly hear each other.

From birth to death, listening and being listened to is the breath of our emotional life.

The rhythmic sound of the mother's heartbeat provides the first sensory stimulation an infant receives. At birth, loud noises and falling are the two primal fears. Gentle sounds and warm enveloping arms are the first sources of security. Listening remains the basic channel for sensing emotions and reading the feeling tone between oneself and another all throughout the stages of life. It is usually the last sense to remain when a stroke cuts off sight, speech and smell. Hearing communicates deep feeling to the heart of a person at any age.

Morning breaks. At the first sounds from the nursery the mother enters and begins the daily greeting ritual. Cooing, talking, testing for wetness or dryness, holding, stroking, reassuring and calling the child by name. This is the beginning of what will be a constant human need for the rest of life. We humans have a central need for consistent recognition and certification. I am known and I am named. I am one with those I love. I am separate and recognized as such. I am part of my family, I am separate and distinct as a person. This is something one knows before he or she knows— that one senses before there are words or thought to name it. We intuit this respect, this reverence for another human person, this blessing that sets us free to be our own unique persons. The most visible experience of it comes to us through listening. When another hears us it is an actual occasion of being honored, valued, respected as a person in our own right, an agent whose actions deserve notice, attention and response.

Being heard is so close to being loved that for the average person they are almost indistinguishable. To say something you value deeply to another and to have him or her value it equally by listening to it carefully and appreciatively is the most universal way of exchanging social interest or demonstrating affection.

To Understand: Hear Each Other

"I'd like a hamburger and a glass of milk," the six-year-old said to the waitress.

"He'll have the child's portion of salisbury steak with mixed vegetables," the mother said, ignoring the boy and ordering for him.

"And what would you like on your hamburger?" the waitress asked.

Surprised, the boy looked up at her with puzzled, then brightening, eyes. "Just ketchup," he said.

After she left the table the boy turned to his mother. "You know what?" he said. "She thinks I'm real."

A child may be the object of much affection and still not be heard as a real person. When the assumption is, "Children are to be seen but not heard," the interchange necessary for maturing is cut off. When the family rule is, "No talking back," two-way communication is forbidden from the crucial moments of conflict where mutual interchange is most important. The response called "talking back" usually occurs when the child responds with the same tone of voice just used by the parent. Children give parents what the parents ask for, not always what they think they are asking for, but what they really are. When a child is heard and understood, the two-way parent-child communication provides a basis for the loving firmness and respectful control that is the mark of good parenting.

Within each human person there is a deep need to be heard as a real person, a person of importance who merits attention and respect. Tragically many marital contracts, family systems, and community practices omit certain persons from notice as significant people who deserve a hearing upon request. These marriages, families or communities operate by the myth that some people are important and deserve attention; others are insignificant and can appropriately be ignored. So certain persons can command the floor at will, others cannot demand a hearing unless special circumstances qualify them to be heard.

A person who is considered a part of the landscape will be heard when in extreme crisis or when he or she inadvertently becomes a witness to some tragedy that affects more "important people." Otherwise the person is a non-person, a background to be assumed, not a foreground to be perceived.

A woman who is seen as a silent partner may be

presumed a part of the wallpaper until she summons the courage to demand a hearing. A man who is withdrawn may be seen as uninterested in the family or uninvolved in its life. As he is bypassed more and more frequently, he moves out of the action and becomes a silent support. Both the over-talked and the under-talker participate in this conspiracy of silence matched with wordiness.

A relationship is as good as its communication is mutual. A family is as healthy as its interest in each member is equal. A community is as wholesome as its communication channels are effective in guaranteeing an equal hearing to each person. To open the channels of hearing and being heard is the crucial first step in clearing communications, clarifying covenants and creating genuine community.

To Understand: Hear Differences

"Obviously you were lying when you said you loved me this morning. How could you be so angry at me after what you promised me?"

"That's how I felt then, I'm angry now."

"But you can't be both. I could never say things like you just said if I really loved you."

"Look, when I feel close I think I could never feel anything but love. Then I get mad. And for a few minutes I wish I had never seen you."

"I can't understand how you can be two such different persons. I never treat you like that. If I say I love you I won't be talking hate an hour later."

She, an even-tempered person who controls feelings and watches her words carefully, cannot understand how he can swing so widely from love to disgust, and speak so affectionately one moment and be enraged the next. Judging him, by

"Of course I'm listening, now what was that you said?"

* * *

"I've had enough of this business about my not really
hearing you, so shut up about it!"

* * *

"I understood every word you said but not a single
sentence."

* * *

"How do you take it, listening to others all day, hearing
their frustrations with empathy, never tiring, how do you do
it?"
"Listen? Who listens?"

* * *

"Oh cut it out. Now you're deliberately listening just to
confuse me."

comparison with herself, he seems double-tongued, deceitful.

He, with an emotional temperament that can swing from intense devotion to immense anger, can make no sense out of her steady and unvarying response to him. Judging by himself she is so perfect, so controlled, so "right" that he can't help feeling guilty in comparison.

Each hears the other through the filter of his or her own personality. When calm they can see many of the differences in each other, but when in conflict they each judge the other by the self, so the other is weighed and found wanting.

Since no human being hears another except through the self, or understands another except by some comparison with herself, the temptation to see others as virtually like the self must be resisted as tensions rise.

People are so different in tastes, in feelings, in hopes. Yet this most obvious of facts is so insistently denied by people, particularly by those who are most close. The thought that another differs in preferences, values, perspectives is seen as a threat, an attack, a challenge to continuing relationships. Marital partners refuse to see the differences as though what is not seen does not exist. Parents blind themselves to the growing uniqueness of a teenager as if what is not noticed will not happen.

Our differences shape the way we face and meet the world. Where one person is fascinated by the outer world of experience, another is intrigued by the inner world of ideas. While one trusts his hunches, the other is strictly facts. Where one judges by feelings, the other insists on strict logic.

We vary so greatly that we can be an almost endless source of novelty and surprise to each other if we mature as listeners. To come to understand another as different from the self presupposes that a good deal of personal growth has taken place. When one comes to know the difference between self and other and can see the other person as the unique being he or she has become, then one has made a long stride toward maturity.

To mature as a listener is to prize the distinctiveness of each person; to listen for the otherness, to respect that uniqueness without attempting to gloss it over, to see the difference without retouching it to match one's own image. To truly listen is to see the other as distinct from myself, especially in those aspects I am tempted to assume are the same without question.

You are you. Nothing in you is identical to me. I want to hear you with all your surprises.

To Understand: Hear the Similarities

John is inaccessible. Cold, detached, aloof.

Jim, his brother, is a people person, hardly ever alone.

—Yet they are clearly brothers.

Alex is abstract, brilliant, head in the clouds.

Albert is concrete, cautious, slow in thought.

—Yet they have so much in common.

Ann is assertive, firm, decisive, demanding.

Alice is passive, yielding, accommodating, easily led.

—Yet they are surprisingly alike.

Between any two humans there are similarities worth hearing, exploring, understanding.

Peter is a rapist, with hate for and obsession with women.

Lisa is sultry and seductive with an insatiable need to control.

George is a time-bomb. His concealed rage

erupted and his wife died.

Elsie is a kvetch, constantly nagging, bitching, backbiting.

They are all like you. They are all like me. We are not different species. They have the same drives, needs, wants as we, only some of them much more so.

There is nothing in another that is foreign to me. Everything present in every other is also within me, at the very least, in the seed impulse, in the potential emotion, action or reaction. I need not reject any person as beyond understanding. There are no impossible people, only difficult ones.

We have so much in common as persons. The life pilgrimage awakens the same basic needs for trust and acceptance, for saying yes and saying no, for play and imagination, for the abilities to work, to choose, to be intimate, to be productive, and to integrate all these into a pattern called wisdom. We search for the same values. We cannot live without *hope*. We become a self through *will*. We venture into life with *purpose*. We strive for some *competence*. We search for *identity*. We long for *love*. We learn to *care*. We discover *wisdom*. We share these steps and stops along the life pilgrimage with every other human. The variations of outcome at each step are as many as there are humans. Each is a unique constellation created by innumerable conscious and unconscious choices. Yet each of us has made the journey of human growth and development, touching at the same basic need points, often making directly opposite choices with sometimes tragically different outcomes, but the similarity remains.

Although it may seem strange at first hearing, most difficulties arise not from our differences but from our similarities. Our differences often

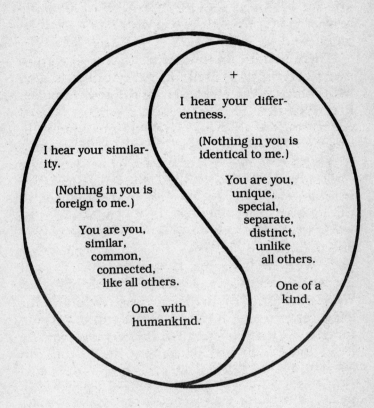

+

I hear your differentness.

(Nothing in you is identical to me.)

You are you,
unique,
special,
separate,
distinct,
unlike
all others.

One of a
kind.

I hear your similarity.

(Nothing in you is foreign to me.)

You are you,
similar,
common,
connected,
like all others.

One with
humankind.

Diagram 1

attract, complete, complement each other; our similarities grate, irritate and frustrate us.

When a fault in you provokes anger in me, then I know that your fault is my fault too. If I have made peace with this same area within myself, my anger will not be aroused by the sight of it in you. But when I hear you saying the very things I hate to hear from myself, I feel inner turmoil.

The similarities may often be in how we act toward each other, not in what we actually say. For example I may say, "I'm sick and tired of your always being so judgmental; you're forever cutting me down in a cranky way." Note who is being judgmental, cutting and cranky! Or I may excuse myself for the very things I dislike in you and reveal it in the act of pointing out your problem. For example, "I'm just being firm in a very responsible way but you are being obstinate, opinionated, even pigheaded." Our similarities are revealed in the way I excuse even as I accuse.

When listening, the similarities can serve as a bridge to cross over and explore the excitement of our differences. Or they can be a wall which shuts out my seeing you accurately. Recognizing the features in which we resemble I may assume that you are like me in other parts too. I may dislike you where I see you as like me—only more so—on the parts I dislike, or less so on the parts of myself I invest with pride. I want to appreciate our similarities, and doubt them, examine them, delighting in discovering your and my uniqueness.

To Understand: Hear All of Each Other

"I must have become invisible or unimportant or something like that at about 70," Jacob reports. "At least people began speaking to me with the kind of comments that needed no response."

"How are we feeling today?"

"My you are looking well."

"And I found that my responses were not heard or did not matter. I gave up the attempt. There is so much to express, but who will listen? Some days I am full of loneliness, reevaluating old hurts, looking for a way to make peace with past conflicts, trying to understand my life. That's when I need to talk. My family is quite willing to hear my happy side, but no one has time for me while I sort out some of the events that really matter."

Deep within our humanness is a profound need to be heard and understood, understood not in part but as a whole. When only a portion of the person is heard, the unknown and unrecognized side presses for attention. Each person deserves to be heard as a whole, to be wholly seen by at least two or three significant others in a lifetime, to be understood not just in part, but as a self of many parts.

Like many aging persons, Jacob, the man just quoted, is doing life-review work, the retelling, reviewing and reintegrating of a lifetime of living. The need to share this process with someone else grips at his soul, but the opportunity to enter into this dialogue with another who will listen deeply does not come his way. If someone is willing to hear both his happiness and his sadness, his gratitude and his resentment, his faith and his despair he may begin to feel understood. Both poles, the positive and the negative, are present in the whole person, although he may be almost totally unaware of one pole. Years of being rewarded for sharing only nice feelings, tactful words, or acceptable responses may so school a person to be sweet and gentle at all times that the negative feelings are submerged, denied, and for-

He is quick, clear, certain.	I am slow, careful, tentative.
He trusts his evaluations.	I constantly question mine.
He assumes he understands.	I doubt if I truly comprehend.
He is confident of the facts.	I suspect there are other facts.
He is dismayed when the fact fails.	I am confirmed when the fact fails.
He then doubts his senses.	I then approve my senses.
He is confused in understanding.	I am understanding my confusion.
He becomes cynically hopeless.	I become cynically hopeful.

How we differ!
We are mirror images.
We each need the other.

gotten. Even when a person has lived a life of careful gentleness, kindness, and avoidance of conflict, the reverse memories will come back for review.

Or the irritable and touchy personality that offers constant criticisms and complaints may have a tender, fearful pole that has never been heard. To draw it out so that both sides are put into words, both sides are clarified in expression to another, both sides gain respect.

In spite of the person's attempts to keep one half of human experience hidden, it will show its face in the communications shared. When another hears the side that is in the shadows, a deep sense of joy wells up from within. Often tears mark the moment of being heard in a new way. They are tears of reunion, as the unknown side of the self is set free to welcome the well-known. As the forgotten pole emerges from silence and finds itself heard, the fears evoked may be intense, the self-rejection immediate, the shame and embarrassment intimidating. The listener can choose to hear the whole person.

You are compounded of more than one side. You are complex with many faces, many poles, many interlocking and interrelating parts. I want to hear all of you, appreciate the many sides of you, come to know the whole community of selves that live within you. To understand you I want to hear from all of you.

To Understand: Hear Myself, Hear the Other

I know
you think you understand
what you thought I said,
but I'm not sure
you are aware

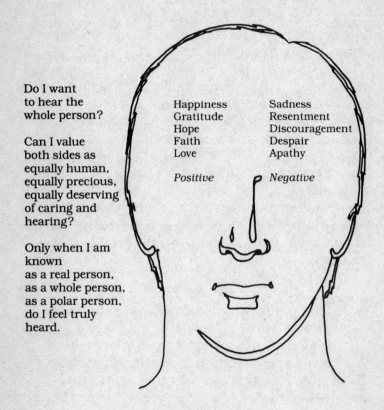

Do I want
to hear the
whole person?

Can I value
both sides as
equally human,
equally precious,
equally deserving
of caring and
hearing?

Only when I am
known
as a real person,
as a whole person,
as a polar person,
do I feel truly
heard.

Happiness   Sadness
Gratitude   Resentment
Hope   Discouragement
Faith   Despair
Love   Apathy

Positive   *Negative*

Diagram 2

that what you heard
is not what
I meant.

To hear your meanings I must first hear mine. My expectations will contribute significantly to what I admit and how I interpret it. I may hear only what I thought you would say, what I want you to say, what I was afraid you might say, and not what you really did say.

If I am to hear you I must also hear me. The more immediately I know the meanings I assign to words, the more accurately I can recognize the meanings you are intending.

To listen accurately to self and other requires a clear recognition of the intimate yet separate relationship that exists between meanings and words. This relationship can be clarified by frequently reminding oneself of the following:

1. *Meanings are in persons, not in words.* "Words don't mean, people mean," as Lewis Carroll observes in the dialogue between Humpty-Dumpty and Alice.

2. *Meanings are not transmitted in oral communication, just oral and visual signals*—sounds, words, pauses, tones, omissions, facial expressions, gestures, posture, even respiration and perspiration.

3. *Meanings which a listener attaches to the signals are based on inferences, hunches, not on facts.* I have only an inkling of your meaning. I make the best guess possible and check it out.

4. *The word is not the meaning just as the wrapper is not the chocolate*; the word is not the object it names just as the photo is not the person; the word is not the experience expressed just as my story is only a small part of that moment of history.

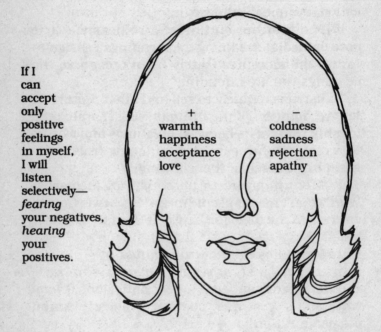

If I
can
accept
only
positive
feelings
in myself,
I will
listen
selectively—
fearing
your negatives,
hearing
your
positives.

+
warmth
happiness
acceptance
love

–
coldness
sadness
rejection
apathy

Diagram 3

5. *Communication is a meeting of meanings.* When your meanings meet my meanings across the bridge of words, and the overlap is sufficient to satisfy us both, then we have achieved co-meanings.

6. *My meanings will never perfectly match your meanings.* Even in an intimately shared, mutually appreciated, truly understood communication, our meanings are uniquely our own.

The meaning intended will only partly approach the meaning invited by the listener. Knowing this, speaker and spoken to must take equal responsibility to match meanings.

In good communication the intent equals the impact. Rare as this seems, it must still be the goal of every communication. My intent, filtered by my expectations—emotions, needs, hopes, fears—gets put into words. These words, filtered by your expectations—emotions, needs, hopes, fears—register an impact on you the listener. When, after passing through these dual filters, the impact is still reasonably close to the original intent, clear communication is occurring.

The speaker carries a responsibility to clarify the message and to seek to make the intended message impactful in accord with the true intentions. He or she is not responsible for the listener's filter or the inferences that are made because of it. To say, "I just dish it out, if the other doesn't get it, that's his problem, or if she misunderstands me, that's her responsibility," is a cop-out. Every speaker must sort out the meanings and clarify the message to be concise and clear.

The listener is responsible to check out the message heard until certain that the impact felt truly matches the intent meant. Good listening is a process of doubting one's own meanings, of then giving the other the shadow of that doubt until it is blazingly clear what the intentions actually are. To say, "I don't need to hear any more, I know what you meant and no amount of your explaining will help," is to drop out too soon in the communication process.

I want, through the puzzling screen of our human filters, to hear your intended message. I will seek to suspend judgment until I have heard your meanings; I will reexamine my own meanings before I assume they are the same as yours. I will listen openly to your meanings whether they are shortchanged by the words you select or inflated by the expressions you choose. I want to hear the you that you mean to mean.

Good communication is co-perception, it is two persons seeking to perceive something in the same way, with the same meanings. Impossible as it is, it is still worth the pursuit. Though the end may never be gained, the journey is rewarding enough without achieving the final goal. Good communicators have learned to love the process without despairing when the end is not realized. Co-meaning, the goal of good listening, is never reached. Co-perception, the focus of careful attending, is never attained. Communication, the purpose of faithful listening, is never complete. But the benefits, the rewards, the values gained en route are worth it all.

I want to hear you. I want to be heard. I want to understand you. I want to be understood.

For Exploration in the Bible

One of the most profound teachers of right relationships who is ordered by what he calls "the

600,000
words
are
available
in the English
language.

Of these,
an educated adult uses
2,000.
And the most used
500
have according to
standard dictionaries
14,000
different definitions.

Each common word
must be used to cover
a wide range of "meanings."

This pitifully small number of symbols
must describe the infinite richness
of your and my experiences.

(Some words have 100 or more different meanings.)

royal law, you shall love your neighbor as yourself,"
is James. Note his words on listening and on
speaking.

Because the section of James's writings which
speaks of the tongue symbolizes the whole of
human communication, I have chosen to paraphrase his words to catch this central and often
overlooked thrust.

1. *On Listening*
Know this, my beloved brethren.
Let every man be quick to listen,
slow to speak, slow to anger.
For human rage does not achieve
the righteous-justice which is the will of
God. . . .
Who is wise and understanding among you?
By his good life let him show his works
in the meekness of wisdom. . . .
The wisdom from above
is first genuine, then peaceable,
gentle and open to reason,
full of mercy and evidences of goodness
without uncertainty or insincerity.
And right relationships grow
from the seeds of peace
planted by those who make peace
(see Jas. 1:19,20; 3:13,17,18).
2. *On Speaking*
We all make many mistakes
and the most difficult thing to master
is communication.
To communicate rightly is to live rightly also.
As a small bit can direct a mighty horse,
as a small rudder can steer a great ship,
as a small spark can light a terrible forest fire,

as a small word can corrupt a person,
so it is with evil communication.
We can tame all the rest of creation
but we cannot tame
the treachery, evil and deception
that is always present
in human communication.
The same words can be heard
as either blessing or cursing.
The same mouth can speak in appreciation or
rejection.
As a spring is either fresh or salt,
as a tree grows its natural fruit,
so must we communicate
in clarity, purity and simplicity
(see Jas. 3:3-12).

For Personal Growth

These 10 statements may assist you in measuring how you feel about both sides of yourself as well as about both sides of the person you are seeking to hear.

	Usually	Sometimes	Neutral	Occasionally	Rarely
1. I am deeply concerned when someone has a poor opinion about me.	—	—	—	—	—
2. I do not want others to know when I feel disgust, impatience or hatred toward them.	—	—	—	—	—
3. I keep my feelings of sadness, resentment, discouragement or depression to myself.	—	—	—	—	—
4. I immediately think of advice to offer when someone shares with me feelings					

In Good Communication—Intent Equals Impact.

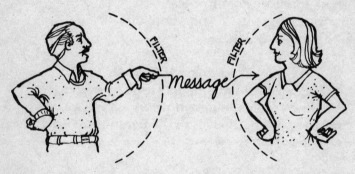

The speaker is responsible
to clarify his message,
to make his impact
equal his intent.

The hearer is responsible
to check out the message
to be sure the intent meant,
matches the impact felt.

Diagram 4

of sadness, discouragement
or despair.   — — — — —

5. I feel deeply hurt, cut to the
quick if someone criticizes
me, scolds me, puts blame
on me.   — — — — —

6. I feel a deep need to never
criticize another directly,
no matter how much I
object to his or her behavior.   — — — — —

7. I feel like someone is rejecting me totally if he dislikes
a part of me, or like he is
dismissing me completely if
he does not like my work or
performance.

8. I doubt if it is possible to
critique a part of a person
without his hearing it as a
total rejection, or her feel-
ing it as a personal attack.   — — — — —

9. I doubt if I am as emotion-
ally healthy as most people
because I have more nega-
tive feelings than others
seem to have.   — — — — —

10. I am really grateful that I do
not have the same impulses
to feel angry, unhappy,
resentful, or discouraged
that others have to face.   — — — — —

If your check marks fall mostly to the left, this indicates that you likely hold a lower view of yourself than is appropriate—that is, you are undervaluing yourself and this leads you to suspect or mistrust others in the same way. If your checks are more to the right, then you are tending to see self and other as equally worthful, trustworthy in the depths, able to accept and use criticism wisely without interpreting it as a total comment on the whole self, and open to value both sides of emotion, intention and experience.

Reread the test and set rumors afloat in your unconscious spaces by answering a firm NO to each item. Be aware of your own thoughts, feelings, impulses as you do this. What can you learn about yourself from this experience? What can you put to work *for* yourself from this exercise?

For Dyadic or Group Process

1. Share a secret from each of your inner sides with the other person(s) by finishing the following lines.
   a. One of the positive feelings I often have, but I do not reveal to you, is . . .
   b. One of the negative feelings I sometimes experience but do not admit is . . .

Respond to the other person(s)' statements with appreciation while asking, "Could I appreciate that quality within myself?" Or, "Could I accept, admit, share that same feeling with another?"

2. "To understand: hear myself, hear the others."

Turn to the six propositions on meanings and words (pp. 25-27) and debate them pro and con.

Have one person take the "Resolved—pro" position, the other the "Resolved—con" position, and appoint the others to serve as a jury.

When the debate has run its course, both persons (if you are doing this in a dyad) or the jury review the ways in which the propositions were proven or disproven by the debate itself, not by the arguments you presented but by what actually happened as you competed, contradicted and communicated. Share what you discover personally from the experience that will sharpen your awareness of how meanings are covered, uncovered, or discovered in conversation.

3. "In good communication, intent equals impact."

Finish the following lines to share some of your presuppositions about communicating:

    a. "Don't judge me by what I say, judge me by what I _____ ."

    b. "I know what my intentions were, so where did you get the idea that _____ ?"

    c. "I am responsible for what I say, I am not responsible for _____ ."

    d. "I am responsible to sharpen what I say, you are responsible to _____ ."

    Now discuss the wisdom from your communication experiments in life that help you in working through these intent-impact discrepancies.

Each person is a unique individual
and thus experiences each situation distinctively.
To really hear him, his own experience,
no matter how different from others,
is the most essential thing to strive for.
Herein each individual is unique,
even though much of his message
may have a familiar ring.
Abraham Schmitt[3]

I feel like a terribly slow learner
in acknowledging that only in recent years
have I come to learn
that listening is a primary way
by which I can become a significant person
in my own eyes and in the eyes of others.
And I must continually relearn it.
Earl Koile[4]

2 ▪ Attending
"Try me again, I'm listening."

Fifteen minutes ago the lawn mower overturned on the hill in our front yard, seriously injuring Nancy's foot. After rushing her to the emergency room of the Goshen Hospital I am standing in the hall waiting for the surgeon's report on whether the toes can be saved. A friend approaches and I pour out the story of the accident. Just as I am about to share my feelings of inner turmoil the other interrupts to tell of two similar accidents.

At that moment I don't want to hear about the pain of persons not present. I want to share my own. Overloaded with worry, concern and empathy for Nan's suffering, all my channels are in use. The information is coming at me, but I am not making use of it. I am hearing it and dismissing it. My only recall at this moment is of my frustration at being told two stories. The content is gone since I refused admittance. Overwhelmed by the trauma Nancy was experiencing and flooded by my concern for her, I was deaf to another's words.

Listening virtually ends when I am overwhelmed by stress, overloaded with tasks or so overinvested in my own concerns that I have little room to entertain another.

To hear another I must make room within

myself to admit the other's words and meanings. When I am filled with excitement or exhaustion I am not available to another. Listening requires an opening of my inner world to receive another. Making room within myself requires a series of steps, taken in part or (in effective listening) attempted as a whole. The steps toward truly hearing another include: (1) a willingness to give another my attention, (2) an openness to perceive the other's views and values, (3) a readiness to suspend judgment or evaluation, (4) a patience to wait for the other's own expression of his or her own thoughts and feelings, (5) a genuineness of empathy that seeks to take the other's position for the moment, to see the world as the other sees it, and (6) a commitment to work toward a dialogue that enriches us both.

The first step is the step of *presence*. If I choose to be present with another, I am recognizing and admitting the other's presence. We are now available to each other.

The second step is *attention*. Opening one's mind to give an evenly, hovering attention to the person, the situation, the message, the voice tone, the feeling tones, the whole self.

The third is *authentic interest*. As I choose to enter the other's world and to see it as he or she sees it I am trying on the other's perceptions to appreciate them and value them as having an integrity of their own, whether I agree with them or not.

Fourth is the *suspension of judgment*. In valuing the integrity of another's perspective I am not sacrificing my own, but suspending the application of my values and the expression of my differences until it is evident that I have truly understood.

Fifth is *patience*. Any attempt to hurry the other, any offer to complete the sentence, any generosity in supplying ideas or words to fill in temporary blanks, any tendency to embellish the other with insights of my own takes away from the full message presented.

Finally, a *commitment to work* toward a mutual, reciprocal dialogue seeks to move the conversation toward an equal exchange of views and values. In dialogue, listening achieves its most present, open, interested, acceptant and trusting expression.

Each of these steps removes or reverses the most common obstacles to hearing others, obstacles created by the highly selective process we use in gathering information. As these are reduced, then we can take new steps toward more effective listening.

Selective Services

With more than 400 selling impressions a day bombarding the average North American, an inner early warning and screening system against this pushy persuasive world is indispensable. The answer is selectivity.

Selective exposure limits the amount of signals coming in by eliminating many of the possibilities. There are TV channels, magazines, books, plays, persons, friends, perhaps even family members that can be dealt with by avoiding or evading any exposure to that person or source.

There are people in my community, students in my classroom, colleagues on the faculty where I teach that I may pass by unless I choose to make contact. Each of us is selecting—consciously or unconsciously—the persons with whom we will

Attending Is a Willingness to Hear

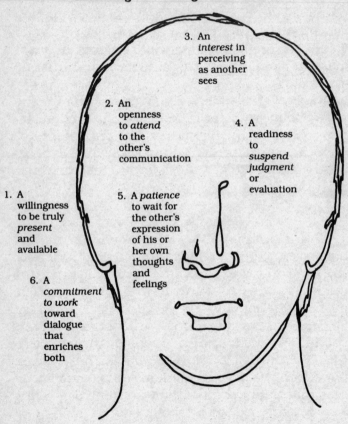

3. An *interest* in perceiving as another sees

2. An openness to *attend* to the other's communication

4. A readiness to *suspend judgment* or evaluation

1. A willingness to be truly *present* and available

5. A *patience* to wait for the other's expression of his or her own thoughts and feelings

6. A *commitment to work* toward dialogue that enriches both

Diagram 5

interact. The narrow selectivity of my, their, your exposure to each other rules out real listening opportunities.

Selective attention screens the data offered without any conscious choice. When a negative attitude is held toward another, any positive data may be automatically ignored or any friendly input from that source may be totally missed. When standing in a circle of people, or sitting in a group, I can become aware of the high selectivity of my attention. I unconsciously zero in on some persons, am less aware of others. I automatically attend to the parts of their conversation I value, I dismiss and miss the parts that impress me less.

Selective perception takes place because I do not see important data which is there before my eyes. I do not hear words, emotions, meanings that are obvious to another but oblivious to me. I see what I am willing to see, hear what I am able to hear. I may see what isn't there or may fail to see what is there. For example, the threat to my leadership of a small group which is implied by a side remark of one of the participants misses me completely. I am absorbed in expressing my view of the group's task. Later as I listen to a tape of the session I hear a totally different message than I could perceive an hour before. I had tuned out the minority and was responding to those who agreed with my concern.

Selective retention edits my memories. I find I tend to recall comments that were rewarding or consistent with my wants and views. I forget those that did not fit or support my assumptions. Memory is the greatest editor of all, and it discards major pieces of information while treasuring trifles. When I try to work through an unresolved conflict that is only an hour old, I find my memory—which I present as though it were complete, perfect and unretouched—is quite different from my partner's—which I can see is partial, biased and clearly rewritten. We both have selective memories.

Selectivity is an asset. It saves us from being overloaded with stimuli, overwhelmed with information, overtaxed with demands from a humming, buzzing environment.

Selectivity is also a liability. If I deny that it is taking place there will be much that I don't see, and I won't see that I don't see. If I pretend I saw it all, understood it all, recall it all, there will be many times when I will argue in vain or cause intense pain in relationship with my inability to hear the other whose point of view is equally good, although probably as partial as my own. We each—even at our best—see in part, understand only in part, and recall only a small part.

Since each person's blend of these "selective-filters" differs from every other's, we are each unique, intriguing, at times puzzling, but always worth hearing out. Because selectivity is in universal use and its variations seem almost infinite, the following catalogue of hearing disorders is at best approximate. Adapt them to describe your listening blocks. Adjust them to match your inner obstacles that serve as mental filters, screens or shields.

Ruling Out the Speaker

"He has nothing new to say. I'm not interested in conversation; count me out."

The first line of listening defense frequently eliminates persons in toto. By ruling out a speaker, one has reduced the number of inputs and eliminated the necessity of hearing that per-

Selective Services
(Safeguard sanity
but limit listening.)

Selective Exposure
(I make contact
with some people;
I flow by others
without notice.
How? Which? Why?)

Selective Attention
(I attend to some parts of
another's communication; I
ignore or screen out parts
which I dislike or which disagree with my beliefs.
When? Which? Why?)

Selective Perception
(I perceive some things that
I expected to find only to
discover they weren't actually there. I saw what I
wanted to see. How? When?
Where? Why?)

Selective Retention
(I recall in part—usually the
rewarding, consistent parts
which match my bias—and
I forget many parts—often
the parts which were puz-
zling and inconsistent with
my views. Which? When?
Why?)

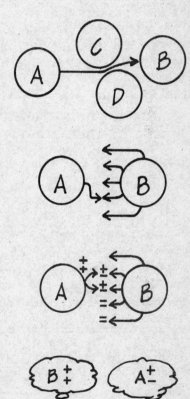

Diagram 6

son's perspective with its potential conflicts or contrasts with my own.

Finish the line: "I do not listen to . . ." (liberals, conservatives, communists, fundamentalists, divorced people, old people, homosexuals, kids, actors, TV preachers, etc.). Now that you've found a few speakers that you rule out without need of conscious thought, check closer to home.

Finish the line: "I tune out . . ." (my son, my work associate, my garrulous sister, my cranky neighbor, etc.).

Ruling out persons ("He's of no interest to me.") cuts off listening before it can begin. A judgment about the whole person I am encountering now has been made on the basis of past experience ("She never has anything new to say; she's a recorded announcement."), so I am blind to the present and have ruled out the other's presence. To rule you out is to say, "As a rule you are not worth hearing. So I will live by the rule that we are to coexist but not contact." I resent that rule when imposed by others. I can refuse that rule when I find it in myself.

I want to give every other the same opportunity I want for myself: that is, the privilege of being present in the present. I am not my past. I am who I am in this moment. Hear me now before you say no. You are not your past. I want to hear you as the you you are now.

Reaching a Premature Conclusion

"I've heard enough to know where you're going with this argument; in fact, I've heard it all before."

Often in mid-argument one has heard enough to reach a tentative conclusion about the other's point of view. If this hunch on what the other

Blocks to Attending

Ruling out the speaker	"He's of no interest to me." "She has nothing to say, why listen anyway?"
Reaching a premature conclusion	"I've heard enough to know where he's going with this argument. I've heard it before and it's all wet."
Reading in expectations	"I know what you're going to say, I can finish your sentence when you pause, I can read you like a book."
Reading out threats	"I know you didn't mean that, you couldn't have said it, you didn't say it."
Rambling or racing ahead	"You trigger a whole flood of thoughts, and one idea leads to another. I've left you; I'm now miles away."
Rehearsing a response	"I am preparing what I want to say. I'm just waiting till you pause so I can break in. . . ."
Reacting to trigger words	"I didn't hear a word you said after you called my child a 'kid.' Goats have kids, have you no respect?"
Responding with evaluation	"The way you say it is (a) clever, (b) creative, (c) crude, (d) contradictory, and I am more interested in the style or the lack of it than in what you are actually saying."
Rejecting the person or personality	"You come on too strong. I don't like authoritarian personalities; I don't need to listen further."

means is tested out and corrected by the other's further statements, it serves as a useful tool to get an accurate picture of the other's perspective. When I assume that the part I have caught represents the whole, then I may stop listening, often just before the crucial point is offered.

Prejudging a communication as uninteresting or unimportant lifts the burden of listening off one's shoulders and frees the attention to wander elsewhere. But two persons are being cheated: the other is not being given a fair hearing, and the listener is being deprived of what may be useful information. I want to cancel all advance judgments—prejudgements—and recognize them for what they are, prejudices. I want to hear the other in a fresh, new way with whatever energies I have available.

Reading in Expectations

"I already know what you're going to say. I can finish your sentence when you pause. I can read you like a book."

Reading in my expectations can inflate, distort, or completely reverse your meanings.

I may read in the emotions I expect, or more often those I project from my own inner feelings. I read anger in your eyes or in your words. In actuality I am the angry one, and what I will not face in myself I see in your face.

Sadness may be seen as resentment, loneliness as withdrawal, tenderness as weakness. In fact, virtually all the emotions can be mistaken for their reverse, and so frequently are. The listener, feeling the opposite emotion as the speaker, may hear the other as the same as the self.

Reading in motivations is a vain attempt to simplify the complexity of our fellow human's

Expectations

I am afraid that you will be unfriendly . . .

    . . . I will be sensitive to anything which can be perceived as distant, cold, critical or rejecting.

If I expect you to be hostile . . .

    . . . I will see any absence of response or any neutral or slightly negative response as proof of your critical or malicious intent.

If I anticipate your support . . .

    . . . I may interpret silence as acceptance, interest as evidence of approval, the sounds you make to signal that you hear as expressions of agreement.

behavior. When I have a hunch about the other's motives, I will tend to hear it confirmed in everything said. "The other is acting out of malice (hear the edge to the voice?) or out of jealousy (see the envious look in the eyes) or out of selfish greed (notice how often she says 'I')." Reading in intentions impugns motives, incriminates the other on the basis of my suspicions or intuitions. Listening is not only filtered by these projections of one's own hunches, it is frequently brought to a total standstill. I want to check out any hunches I have until you either correct or confirm them. Any hunches on your motives I will seek to cancel or confess so that they will not be barriers to our communication.

Reading Out Threats

"I don't believe you said that. I'm sure you didn't mean what it sounded like. Of course you didn't say it."

While some personalities read out threats that are actually there, others read them in where they do not exist. One man's threat may be another's pleasure, as one's food is another's poison. One person delights in a compliment; another fears it as an obligation, a manipulation as an expectation that one will always do as well or better. Whatever the threat, the listener can tune it out or tone it down by selective attention or retention. It is so easy to miss a key turn of thought or a closing twist of another's comment, and only later to discover that the threat posed—whether positive or negative—was filtered out and lost. I want to hear the other's input, warts and all, threats and all, and then respond by choice, not by instinct or accident.

Reaching a Premature Conclusion—
Reading in Expectations—

—all contribute to the creation of self-fulfilling prophe-cies.

1. As I see puzzling signs or signals on your face or hear them in the edge on your voice,

2. I may assume that all of your feelings are negative or hostile.

3. I react defensively by blaming or offensively by attacking you before you can attack me, or obliquely by withdrawing and cutting off contact before you can reject me.

4. I thus intensify the situation, your frustration increases and what positive feelings existed now decrease.

5. So my original assumption (which was then false) is now confirmed as true. I have created a self-fulfilling prophecy!

Rambling or Racing Ahead

"You trigger a whole flood of thoughts, one idea leads to another. I've left your train of thought, I'm a thousand miles away."

We humans think at about four hundred words a minute, we speak at a fourth of that. This thought-speech time differential creates infinite possibilities for rambling off down a side road suggested by the speaker, or racing toward a finish line the other has not yet neared. Since we can process information when listening far more rapidly than the speaker can put it out, we have the choice of listening creatively by staying with the same topic, and testing, critiquing, supporting, applying the insights, or letting our thoughts wander off to some distant place from which they may never return. When I listen, I want to stay in touch with each step of the speaker's journey and make only short side trips to gather more data that enrich the other's insights or correct and clarify the arguments. I want to arrive at the end of the sentence at the same place and at the same time.

Rehearsing a Response

"I'm preparing a really powerful response. I can hardly wait until you pause so that I can break in."

"We are," as Wendell Johnson noted, "our own most enchanted listeners. No one speaks as well or on such interesting topics as we do. If we could listen just to ourselves, listening would be no problem." The great temptation to listen to our own thoughts and polish them for presentation at the earliest opportunity seduces us away from the other's words to dally with our own. Particularly when the other has said something with which we disagree, it is tempting to rehearse a rebuttal or repair our previous point or create a new response. Meanwhile we have missed whatever the other was offering—perhaps the part which would make our next question unnecessary or our ready argument irrelevant or the clever comment just polished truly superfluous.

When I listen, I want to stay with the other to the end of the point or paragraph.

There will be time enough to share my own point of view. If I fear losing a flash of genius, I can report that honestly rather than tune out the other to do my speech preparation. "Excuse me, a thought just occurred that I'm afraid I'll lose. . ." can be said as a compliment to the other if one returns the conversational serve after expressing the insight.

Reacting to Trigger Words

"I didn't hear a word you said after you called my son a 'brat'; that word has a heavy emotional load for me. Could we start over there?"

"Signal reactions" occur when one hears a word that has become charged with emotions.

"As soon as you said that our country is 'exploiting' third world nations, I knew you were a communist," an angry man once told me. It took us five minutes to launder the word "exploit" before we could proceed, since he had only heard it used by those he considered "the enemy." When a "signal reaction" occurs, the offending word— kids, teenagers, rebels, hippies, women's libbers, honky, nigger, homo, commie, pinko, fundie, hawk, dove—stops or distorts the communication from that point on. The emotional loading can be either discharged by the listener's recognition that a feeling from bad past associations is making noise in the ears, or it can be expressed to the other in recognition that feelings are being ampli-

fied by a bad word choice. When I become aware
that feelings are flaring in response to one of my
inflammatory words I will own it to myself and, if I
cannot cancel the exaggeration, discuss it frankly
with the other. I would like to make peace with my
whole vocabulary so that as few words as possible
have the power to trigger negative emotions.

Responding with Evaluation

"The way you said that was so (a) clever, (b)
insightful, (c) crude, (d) vague, (e) contradictory. I
(do) don't like your style. I (like) resent your manner and I'm so caught by how you're saying it I
don't know what you've said."

Human beings share a common tendency to
respond to others with evaluation first and with
understanding last. Carl Rogers, Eli Porter, Jr.
and associates tested people from various helping
professions to determine which kind of
response—evaluation, interpretation, support,
probing or understanding—was most frequently
given first. They are most commonly given, they
discovered, in that order. *Evaluation* of the person, process, personality, perspective or coping
style came first. *Understanding* of the other, the
most important ingredient in effective listening,
came last.

Evaluating the other is a most effective means
of distancing from his or her problem or unhook-
ing from any inclination or obligation to help. An
evaluation pushes the other away; whether it's an
approval or a disapproval it is asserting the judge's
right to pass judgment. Close-up videotapes of
people in conversation show that the face gives an
unconscious shock signal when an evaluation is
received. A vertical wrinkle appears between the
eyes for a split second as the eyebrows pull

Track Down "Signal Reactions"

When I react to a word you choose or an expression you use, I am hooked by the signal (and what it signifies to me) and I miss the meaning you intended.

Disarm Emotion-Rousing Words

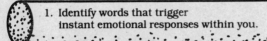

1. Identify words that trigger instant emotional responses within you.

2. Explore the negative experiences you associate with these words.

3. Add additional definitions by recognizing the other meanings it may have for another person.

1. Identify words that trigger instant emotional responses within you.

2. Explore the negative experiences you associate with these words.

3. Add additional definitions by recognizing the other meanings it may have for another person.

DYNAMITE	DYNAMITE	DYNAMITE
I hear: "bitch"	I think: "a dirty, malicious, evil woman, a real dog."	He means: "someone who criticizes freely."
I hear "hippie"	I think: "an unwashed, immoral, irresponsible kid."	She means: "someone who nonconforms freely to oppressive conformity."

Diagram 7

together in the universal sign of anxiety or pain.
As the value judgment is perceived, the face regis-
ters the impact of the vertical words, no matter
how subtle. Knowing that evaluations block effective listening, I want to learn the art of giving
understanding responses until the appropriate
time for evaluations arrives. Often when that time
has come, the evaluations which seemed important earlier are no longer needed.

Rejecting the Person or Personality

"I don't like authoritarian personalities.
There's something about the way you come on
strong that really turns me off. After the first sentence or two I'm no longer listening."

Each personality, except for those who are
monotonously stuck in the middle, has a polar
opposite that tends to both attract and irritate.
Nice guys often resent dominant, controlling
types. Conforming people dislike authoritarians.
Suspicious persons can't stand those who are
ingratiating. Good listeners get exhausted by
those who never listen in return. And even more
frustrating than those who differ from us are
those who are like us. Similarities, not differences, cause most conflicts. When I see the traits
that I am fighting in me expressed so brazenly by
another, I do to them what I've been doing to
myself.

Rejecting the person because I dislike a part of
his or her self-presentation is a mistaking of that
part for the whole. I want to value each person as
worthful whether or not I agree with the whole of
the person or approve of each part of his or her
personality or am attracted to a way of behaving.
Listening is the most elemental language for such
valuing. I want to hear the other for who and what
that other truly is.

Ten Commandments of Listening

Ten Commandments for Hearing

I. *On passing judgment*

Thou shalt neither judge nor evaluate until thou hast truly understood. "Hold it right there, I've heard enough to know where you stand and you're all wet."

I will first understand, then judge. I will suspend judgment, postpone evaluation, defer closure until the other feels heard.

II. *On adding insights*

Thou shalt not attribute ideas or contribute insights to those stated. "If you mean this, it will lead to there, and then you must also mean that."

I will not fill in the gaps with my ideas. I will listen to you, not to my improvements, my embellishments or my supporting data.

III. *On assuming agreement*

Thou shalt not assume that what you heard is what was truly said or what was really meant. "I know what you meant, no matter what you say now. I heard you with my own ears."

I will not assume that the intent in you and the impact on me are one and the same. I will not infer that you said what I heard, think as I thought, meant what I felt.

IV. *On drifting atten-
tion*

Thou shalt not per-
mit thy thoughts to
stray or thy atten-
tion to wander.
"When you said
that, it triggered
an interesting idea
that I like better
than yours."

I will attend to your
words, your feelings,
your meanings. I will
not ramble off, race
ahead, or drop off
asleep.

V. *On closing the
mind*

Thou shalt not
close thy mind to
o p p o s i n g
thoughts, thy ears
to opposite truths,
thy eyes to other
views. "After you
used that sexist
language I didn't
hear another thing
you said."

I will listen to your
whole message, even if
I would rather not hear
it, see it, consider it.

VI. *On wishful hear-
ing*

Thou shalt not per-
mit thy heart to
rule thy mind, nor
thy mind thy heart.
"I just knew you
were going to say
that, I had it fig-
ured all along."

I will avoid wishful
hearing. I will neither
use my ears to hear
what the heart wants
to hear, nor the mind
to filter what the head
will heed.

VII. *On multiple mean-
ings.*

Thou shalt not

I will test both your

interpret words except as they are interpreted by the speaker. "If I were to stop breathing, would I or would I not expire?"

meanings and my meanings until they meet. The content of your words is yours. I want to discover it. The word is the package, the meaning is the contents.

VIII. *On rehearsing responses*
Thou shalt not use the other's time to prepare responses of your own. "I can't wait until you need a breath! Have I got a comeback for you."

I will listen to your full statement without using your time to polish my response or prepare my arguments.

IX. *On fearing challenge*
Thou shalt not fear c o r r e c t i o n , improvement or change. "I'm talking faster and snowing you because I don't want to hear what you've got to say."

I will not be afraid to listen, to learn, to change, to grow. The listener is not inferior, the speaker superior, each enriches the other.

X. *On evading equality*
Thou shalt not over-demand time or fail to claim your own time to hear and be heard. "I

I will respect your right to be equally heard; I will claim my right to be equally heard.

want equal time. I
want you to feel
equally heard."

For Exploration in the Bible

The ability to see, hear, perceive, understand, change and grow is a blend of openness and depth. The greatest of all teachers encountered a rich variety of listeners and non-listeners. His confrontation of the latter as seeing without sight, hearing without recognition, listening without perception stands as some of the sharpest satire of all time. The parable of confrontation has intrigued interpreters for two thousand years. Although there are multiple levels of meaning within the parable, it is helpful to examine it for the level of insight into listening skills. Examine Matthew 13:3-23 for the following:

1. The closed and shallow listener—the beaten path (the hardhead). Exposed to the same as the others, but closed to new insight it is impenetrable, non-receptive, and the new truth is lost. The new thought never sprouts.

2. The open but shallow listener—the rocky soil (the shallow mind). Open to new insight, it grasps the ideas and toys with them but the rocky base frustrates any depth growth. So the new ideas are quickly killed. The new thought never matures by the impervious rocky base.

3. The open, deep but conflicted listener— thorny soil (the divided self). Open to new truth, but indiscriminately hospitable, the thorny soil gives its depth and nourishment to good and bad with equal warmth. The new ideas are added to the already cluttered mind so that they are quickly crowded out, choked off. The new thought never bears fruit.

4. The open, deep and responsive listener—the

good soil (the open mind). Open to new insight, deep in its welcome for truth, the rooting, growth and maturation of new concepts reaches productivity and fruitfulness. The new word heard is fulfilled in thought, feeling and action.

The art of listening responsively and responsibly requires both openness and selectivity, both depth and discrimination. It is hearing and reflecting, listening and deciding. Note how all of these are true at different times in your listening. List the setting in which you tend toward any of these as a dominant style.

"They seeing see not; and hearing they hear not, neither do they understand. . . . "By hearing ye shall hear, and shall not understand; seeing ye shall see, and shall not perceive." Matthew 13:13,14

Blessed are your eyes, for they see, and your ears, for they hear.

For the heart waxes gross, the ears dull of hearing, the eyes closed lest at any time they should see with their eyes and hear with their ears and understand with their heart and should turn and change and be converted and I should heal them. (see Matthew 13:15)

Who hath ears to hear, Let her hear! Let him hear! Let us hear!

For Personal Growth

(Circle the appropriate response to these questions.)

Yes   No   1. Do you listen precisely, seeking to recall the exact words rather than the meanings and ideas?

Yes   No   2. Do you listen tactfully, giving encouragement to others by appearing to pay attention even when you are not?

Yes   No   3. Do you listen selectively, refusing to be bogged down by ideas that are hard to understand?

Yes   No   4. Do you listen intensely, clarifying any confusion immediately, interrupting to straighten out puzzling comments?

Yes   No   5. Do you listen creatively, using your ability to think four times faster than a person usually talks to compare other thoughts or explore other ideas while monitoring the other's conversation?

Yes   No   6. Do you listen economically, turning your attention to other subjects when it seems clear from the speaker's appearance or delivery or use of objectionable words that he or she likely has little interesting to say?

Yes   No   7. Do you listen openly, giving equal attention to the sights and sounds of the situation around you?

Scoring: If you answered *no* to all of the above, then you have learned the optimum listening behaviors.

For Dyadic or Group Process

1. To identify the point of difficulty in attending, each person check the scale in self-evaluation, then compare, discuss, plan for growth.

	weak				strong
a. I am willing to be truly present and available.	1	2	3	4	5
b. I am open to attend another's communication.	1	2	3	4	5
c. I am interested in seeing as the other sees.	1	2	3	4	5
d. I habitually suspend judgment or evaluation.	1	2	3	4	5
e. I am patient in waiting for the other's self-expression.	1	2	3	4	5
f. I am committed to work toward mutual dialogue.	1	2	3	4	5

2. Examine the chart summarizing the most common blocks to effective listening. Pick your top three. Pick your partner's top three as you observe his or her listening process. (If in small group, pair up for this exercise.) Now compare your self-evaluation with the other's observation. Report any learnings which you plan to incorporate into your growth.

3. Examine the five steps of creating a self-fulfilling prophecy. Examine a recent experience of misunderstanding between yourself and some significant other to see if you can trace this cyclical pattern in your responses. Tell the story in concise form, first as a tragedy, "I done her wrong," and then as a comedy, "Look at our game of tag—you're it, now I'm it, etc."

4. Reflect on the "Ten Commandments of Listening." Recognize when, where, how, with what consequences these commandments are broken in your relationship, in your group, in your present discussion. Roleplay the commandment you find most difficult. Reaffirm the appropriate resolutions and plan a way to immediately admit when an old habit of not listening is recurring and to re-express your choice to extend your listening skills or to try out a new behavior. Plan commendations you can offer another as they exhibit new or more effective ways of attending, hearing, responding.

Relationship is dialogue.
Dialogue occurs when one person addresses another person
and the other person responds.
It is a two-way process in which two or more people
discuss meanings that concern them.
To whatever degree one part of the dialogue is lost,
to that degree the relationship ceases to exist.
Reuel Howe[5]

Dialogue goes directly and honestly
to the difference between "me and thee,"
and this requires an immense toughness of self
—for it does combat without going on the defensive.
Paul W. Keller and Charles T. Brown[6]

In a meaningful friendship, caring is mutual,
each cares for the other; caring becomes contagious.
My caring for the other helps activate his caring for me;
and similarly his caring for me helps activate my caring for
*   him,*
it "strengthens" me to care for him.
Milton Mayeroff[7]

3 ■ Hearing

"I want to hear, I want to be heard."

"We've been married for 40 years and never had a cross word between us," the husband said. "All this talk on good communication and fighting fair is a waste of time. All a couple has to do is just decide to live quietly with no trouble."

"How did you do it, not communicating any negative feelings?"

"She always did what I told her."

"And how did it work out for you?" I asked her.

"He always bought me everything I wanted."

A perfect trade. Each demanding little of the other, neither requiring more than the minimum of risk. Both satisfied in the exchange with no need for review—or to move to deeper levels of contact.

No relationship is better than its communication is clear. The health of any relationship—friendship, partnership, marriage—begins in open two-way communication with some quality of equality within it. The more equal, level, mutual the conversation, the higher will be the satisfaction of both participants.

Equal communication presses toward dialogue. As monologue isolates the person in his own world of thought and speech, dialogue opens relationship so that real contact between persons can open mutual understandings at deeper and deeper levels. Communication can be usefully visualized as the contact between superficial levels such as a threat or the exchange of threats to the deepest levels of shared feeling in dialogue.

In stress, in threat situations, in strained relations, in the contract of persons coexisting, or in conversations between people we do not know, we are most likely to meet in the lowest levels of communication. As trust and understanding deepen we move closer as though layer by layer we achieve and utilize gradually more complete pictures of the other's values, intentions and emotions.

For the threat level of communication, I need know, care or feel little for you as a person to lay a threat on you. If all I want is immediate compliance and obedience, then threat is sufficient for the moment even though eventual boomerang effects will sabotage later cooperation.

To move to the bargaining level of communication, I will need to share a common working set of understandings of your and my need or greed. Most important will be a basic trust that this is a trade and not a raid, that the conditions of the exchange will be fulfilled, that what is risked will be gained. Many of our human differences are resolved by offering something for something, a *quid pro quo* agreement, as it is legally termed, in which each stipulates something desired from the other and gives an equal value or concession in return.

For one or both of us to attempt manipulation of the other, either or both persons will need a much more complex picture of the partner's strengths and weaknesses, likes and dislikes, fears and desires. In fact, a rather clear map of the other's behavioral repertoire is intuited, tested and revised by the manipulator in the attempt of matching his or her ploy to the other's play. Manipulation comes in as many varieties as there are ways of attempting to outmaneuver, outsmart, out-dance another—seduction, deception, pretense, shaming, guilt induction, dominance, submission, oppression, martyrdom, teasing or tempting. The plots and counterplots, the hopes of drawing the other into one's game, of playing competing or complementary games weave people into webs of tangled communications. Manipulators get manipulated. No rule of human behavior is more self-evident and yet so unrecognized by the participants. The authoritarian who imposes his will on the submissive person who yields readily, pays in later obligation. The top dog may gain the satisfaction of the immediate goals, but the underdog as often wins in the end a complementary victory by covert means.

To communicate on the level of real persuasion—not the seductive, deceptive or manipulative persuasion forms just examined—requires a fuller appreciation of the other's values, views, priorities, basic beliefs and goals. Persuasion is a co-active process, not a pairing of an active talker and a passive recipient. Both enter into sharing their positions and testing them against the other's. Both may hold deeply to their views and yet extend genuine openness to being confronted by the other and a willingness to consider change. At this level, persuasion shades gradually into mutual, reciprocal dialogue.

1
Threat
Requires little or no understanding of the other, just what the person dislikes or fears.

Cares little about the effect the threat will have on the other as long as he/she submits or obeys.

Overt threats are a clear verbal attack.

Covert threats undermine the other's self-esteem, raise anxiety or imply danger.

2
Manipulation
Each must have some insight into the other's likes and dislikes, strengths and vulnerable points.

Those who manipulate get manipulated. There is usually some joint involvement in manipulation since it takes two to make the game-playing work.

Seduction
Intimidation
Dominance
Submission
Martyrdom
Oppression
Guilt
Induction
Shaming
Deception
Pretense

3
Bargaining
Each now understands what the other wants and what one is willing to offer in an exchange for a quid pro quo.

There must be trust that this is a trade, not a raid, and that all of the agreements and pledges in the exchange will be kept.

4
Persuasion
Each must understand the other's feelings, values, tastes and preferences quite fully in order to persuade.

Persuasion is a co-active process in which both profit. There must be a benefit to both the persuader and the persuadee.

5
Dialogue
Mutual openness and understanding occur as persons seek to fully hear and be heard.

Equal interchange with increasing self-disclosure.

High trust is expressed as each is being genuine, level and free with feelings.

Diagram 8

In dialogue, there is a mutual respect for the other person and his or her freedom to perceive, feel, value and communicate in her own manner, in his own way. Dialogue is a two-way process in which two persons reveal, discuss and extend the concerns that each prizes and now unfolds with the other. There is a mutual process of uncovering and discovering. To communicate in dialogue I must become aware of you—to discover the you being put forward at this moment. I must invite you to be aware of me—to uncover the self I am at this point in time. I must be open to change during our conversation and to share these changes as they are occurring so that we can appreciate the other's flow of thought process as it progresses.

This equal interchange occurs as each feels equally heard by the other. For the one, this may take more of the time and result in many more words as thoughts and feelings are being tested and clarified against the other, who may need less opportunity to speak at that moment even though the conversation calls up the same depth of insight and emotion for review. Neither is seeking to usurp the other's freedom or use the other without voluntary consent, yet each offers the other full use of his or her stance and perspective to complete or correct the views being shared.

Dialogue is a peak experience; it is also a plateau that can be achieved with increasing and sustained regularity as a relationship matures. The ability to move to dialogue at will is the mark of a deepened relationship of proven trust and commitment. It also requires the learning of effective equal communication behaviors and the unlearning of vertical styles of communicating which were taught in the family of origin or caught from the

Levels of Intimacy in Communication

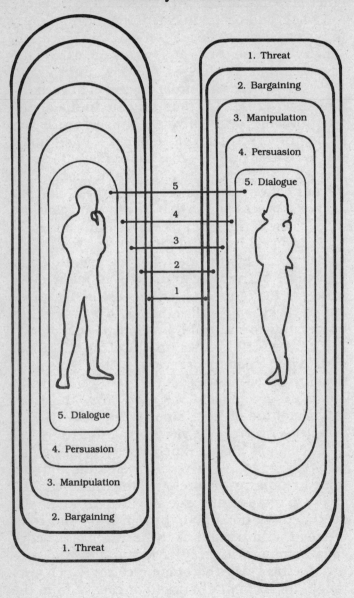

1. Threat
2. Bargaining
3. Manipulation
4. Persuasion
5. Dialogue

5. Dialogue
4. Persuasion
3. Manipulation
2. Bargaining
1. Threat

Diagram 9

world of peers, school, church and work. The art of equal level co-response is gained by many of us through much pain, then lost and regained many times until the freedom to move directly into immediacy with each other at the level of intimacy which both desire becomes a skill of second nature.

In stress we regress back to communication behaviors that we had hoped were forgotten. As anxiety drops, the ability to think, choose, and match our words and intents returns.

As situations change, we move back and forth across the levels of communication. There are appropriate times for the use of threats, though they are far less frequent, we note in hindsight, than we may imagine when swept along by impatience. There are many fruitful times for bargaining which can provide an exchange of favors, change of behaviors, or interchange of materials. Manipulation, as persons mature and grow, undergoes a transformation from deceptive, destructive or parasitic games to openly recognized, creative, mutually pleasurable games of friendly play or intimate celebration. Persuasion becomes more genuine and dialogue more frequent.

Silence takes a new and richer meaning as one learns to move toward dialogue. Silence is violence when used in the threat mode. Foreboding overcontrol and ominous avoidance of each other can speak a thousand threats in a set of the jaw, a shifting of the eyes, a stiffness of the neck.

Silence in bargaining can be either coercion or consent. In manipulation the silent treatment comes into its own as a means of maneuvering without self-revealing. Silence can evoke fears of the unknown: "I am afraid of your silence because of what it could mean—you are bored, you are losing interest, you are making up your own mind without my traveling along, you are choosing the reverse of my hopes, you are about to refuse my guidance, you are in flight from my presence."

Silence in dialogue comes to mean confidence, mutual respect, savoring of the awareness that we are already together, a celebration of mutual trust.

Conscious and unconscious instructions within us guide our uses of silence, misuses of communication and abuses of relationship. These "inner contracts" shape our interactions with others and unless called to awareness, challenged, and the habits reinstructed, can lead us to repeat ineffective behaviors indefinitely. Reinstructing oneself and recontracting with others are the two crucial ways of creating new communication behaviors. To recovenant one's relationships with a single significant other is the most powerful step toward breaking down old patterns and building up a new repertoire of open, level, equal, mutual ways of communicating horizontally.

To better understand the qualities of an equal covenant, examine the following seven clauses with the primary focus being the equal covenanting of a marital relationship. In no way do we mean to imply that the identical principles and processes are not equally appropriate, important, and powerful in singles, siblings, parent-child, co-workers and collegial relationships. Translate, adapt and adjust the concepts and contracts to fit the particular relationship in focus for you as we work through the clauses of equal hearing, ownership, presence, integrity, responsibility, conciliation and wholeness.

I. Equal Hearing

I want to hear. I want to be heard.

Born with an active mouth, rewarded for exercising it often, raised among articulate people, he emerged as a person with something to say even when he had nothing to say. He was destined to fall in love with a girl with beautiful ears. Eloquent in expressing herself, she had early learned to do it concisely, briefly, and often with her eyes or through silence. In early marriage, a predictable and problematic pattern began to emerge. He spoke for both. Had he been confronted with the presumptuousness of his behavior he would only have protested with his desire to be helpful and point out how she looked to him for further explanation or smiled as he took the thread of conversation and carried it for two. Had she been nudged to claim her rights to communication she, like many other "accepting" wives, would have seen it as "the way things are." Only later would she mention the resentment at being taken for granted.

Years passed. Years in which the speaking-for symbolized the ways in which his *dominance* absorbed her energies and her *submission* controlled his. Depressing and being depressed, presuming and feeling consumed, blaming and feeling blamed were buried beneath the niceness, the you-go-ahead-no-you-come-first tact of a united front. Then the pain of unrecognized and unexpressed feelings began to surface. And the first signs of the recreation of the marriage came in the recovenanting of equal communication. It began with her saying, "Stop, I will speak for me"; "Wait, before you go any farther with that 'we,' you speak for you and I'll speak for me."

Innocent pronouns. I, you, we, they—right? No! They are often the most accurate indicators of

I. Equal Hearing

I will claim	I will respect
my right	your right
to be	to be
equally heard.	equally heard.
I am I.	You are you.
I want	I want
to be heard.	to hear you.
(If I yield	(If I usurp
my right to speak,	your right to speak,
if I do not claim	if I use up
my time for sharing,	your time for conversing,
if I do not express	if I do not listen
what I want in equality,	for what you want in
I am squandering	equality,
my privilege of	I am stifling
personhood.)	your privilege of
	personhood.)

what the inner contracts of a marriage really contain. As each spoke for her and himself, each claimed an *I* position from which each could say what "I see, I think, I feel, I want." Equality as persons of worth, insight, preciousness began to be experienced by both. Destructive patterns were redirected toward more constructive ends. Depressing ways of feeling, thinking and speaking were restructured toward expressive and intimate goals.

Ways of communicating which were toxic to both persons, caustic to their attempts at real caring, and unhealthy for their growth in personality and spirituality were at last receiving a much-needed revision called *repentance*.

He discovered that her eloquence, her insight, her gift of words was equally important as his own, and that his need to listen, to respect, to learn was equally a gift. (I can write these words with certainty, for I am he.)

When one person dominates, two people are responsible: the one who overfunctions and the one who allows or contributes to its happening. It takes two to create and continue such a cycle. One can quit.

When two people choose to live on the levels of threat/yielding, bargaining/dickering, or manipulation, they are each responsible, they both deserve each other. Either can invite a move toward equal dialogue.

If I do not claim my right to be equally heard, no one can do it for me. If you do not make full use of your half of a relationship, no other can enter into an equal relationship with you.

So I will claim my privilege of being equally heard with all seriousness. If I passively yield my right to speak even with the intention of being thoughtful, kind and loving, the action is still an act against love. To love another equally is to protect and promote that person's participation in equal conversation and equal communication. To love you as I love myself is to seek to hear you as I want to be heard and understand you as I long to be understood. Acquiescing my part not only indicates a lack of love for the self, it also results in a loss of loving for the other. Such modeling of quiet withdrawal and of silent withholding of feelings is a forceful request for the same from the other. If the other responds by overfunctioning, then my passivity aids and abets in the domination of our time together, even though the conscious motives of "putting the other before myself" be ever so nobly worded in thought and intent.

I am I. I am worthy of being truly heard. You are You. You are valued and I equally value your word.

II. Equal Ownership

He was romantic at heart. He assumed that loving drew two people irresistibly into a union of souls that made misunderstandings—when love was true—unlikely if not impossible. Thus each could fulfill the other's thoughts, feelings, wants, and needs without the tawdry necessity of talking about it. To need to ask was an admission that he had failed in being perfectly attuned to her in loving sensitivity.

She entered relationship with a dream, a dream of being fully understood by a loving person who felt what she felt, wanted what she wanted and would move to fulfill the need before it became a wish.

Thus the lines of ownership for thoughts, feelings and wants became ever more fuzzy and ill-defined. As each took ownership of the joint emo-

II. Equal Ownership

I will claim
my full ownership
for my side
of the dialogue.
I will not
let you speak for me.

(If I do not speak for me,
who can?
If I do not share how I see,
who will?

If I do not disclose what I
feel,

who dares?
If I do not claim ownership

for my experience
of my world
of perceptions, emotions,
volitions,

it will go unowned.)

I will respect
your sole ownership
for your side
of the dialogue.
I will not
speak for you.

(If you do not speak for you,
I cannot.

If you do not share how you
see, I will not.

If you do not reveal what
you feel,
I dare not.
If you do not claim ownership
of your experience
of your world

of perceptions, emotions,
volitions,
it will go unowned.)

tional account, both owned too much and neither owned anything. Both preferred *we* language that presumed the other's loving solidarity. Neither took *I* positions that would risk autonomy. A solidarity composed of two who claim little autonomy becomes a vehicle for one to absorb another.

Although we have illustrated equal ownership from a marital contract, the same respect for ownership is crucial to every other interpersonal dialogue—a friendship understanding, a collegial contract, even a casual contact.

I will claim full ownership for my side of the dialogue. I will respect your sole ownership for your side. I will not speak for you nor will I let you speak for me. Only on those items or issues which express a recent or present contract between us will I use the *we* forms of describing our joint position. On past positions, a more accurate response is to report how I recall the agreement rather than assert "we said, we decided, we thought, we believe." You grow, change, evolve. I move, mature, become more free to see things in a new or more complete light. As I own my experience, I invite your ownership of yours. I welcome your firm claim on your own perspective. Break into my *we* with "I'm ready to report how I see it now." As I feel wedged in by your *we* I will report what I now see.

III. Equal Presence

He was an emotional photographer. He had photographed her at moments of perfect lighting, retouched the shadows, airbrushed the flaws, and penciled in hopes, dreams, fantasies of who she was, what she would become. All unaware he also tinted into the picture the anxieties, fears, and prophecies that were from deep within himself. When he was with her he did not see her, he saw his picture and he responded to glimpses of its beauty or reacted to its distortions.

She was an emotional artist. She had painted a portrait of him from her own inner collection of dreams to be realized and dangers to be evaded. When in his company she was not present or in his presence. The pictures met, the illusions communed, the tapes of recorded expectations blended. At times there were flickerings of reality, flashes of clarity received with both joy and fear. As the ability to sustain this open awareness without reference to the pictures was acquired, bit by painful bit, the joy of immediacy overcame the fear of powerful presence. (I look back on the remembered picture with amused and amazed eyes, for I was he.)

I want to meet you now as the person you truly are and offer the self that I truly am. As I discover parts of the image of you that block my vision like a mosaic of memory shards, I want to clear them away to see you as the growing, changing, surprising person you are.

When we are apart, I will review my memory pictures with appreciation and willfully choose to doubt them before we meet again. When I look into the future I will freely dream dreams of your becoming, and then dispel them as the rumors of change that rise from my hopes for you. You are not your past, I will lay aside my pictures of you. You are not my dreams. I will turn aside from my imaging of you. I want to meet you as you.

When separated for a time I will prize my own freedom to flow in continuing growth, and not feel the urgency to return to what I was in our meeting or the fear to share who I am becoming in your absence. I will prize your opportunity to walk your own path of discovery and meet you at the cross-

III. Equal Presence

I will meet you now
as the person you truly are.
I will stop myself
from speaking to
my image of you.
I cancel the demand
that you be what you were
or become what I want.

(I remember the you of yes-
terday with fondness and
frustration.
You are not your past.
You are who you are now.

I anticipate the you of
tomorrow

with faith and with fear.

You are not my dreams,
you are what you are now.
I want to meet you
as you.)

I will be with you now
as the person I truly am.
I will not be trying
to match or fulfill
your image of me.
I claim the freedom
to change what I was
and to choose who I am
becoming.

(I recall the me I have been
with appreciation and
regret.
I am not my past.
I am who I am here with you
now.

I envision the self I am
becoming
with trust and with trem-
bling.
I am not my hopes,
I am what I am now.
I want to be known
as the I I am.)

ing point with surprise and the excitement of new relating, for there will be a newness about you if I will see it. I recognize that I will, at best, know you only in part; I welcome this limitation to my knowing since it awakens the possibility of unending novelty in our relationship.

Paul Tournier says it concisely in *To Understand Each Other.* "If you think that you know your wife or your husband, it is because you have given up the real attempt to discover him. The difference between the image you have made of him, and what he really is, will grow ever deeper."[8]

I want to see you as you are, be seen as I am.

IV. Equal Integrity

"In a good family one never says, 'I want.' That is the sign of self-centered immaturity. When people love each other, each looks out for the other and senses what the other needs without anyone needing to ask. If you have to ask for something, it is not worth it."

The earnest young man who took this position in a workshop discussion was defending the practice of each sensing the other's needs as the undeniable evidence of authentic love as well as the highest expression of a virtue called unselfishness. He is not alone; in many groups there are more who live by his perspective than those who mistrust mind reading.

For many, the willingness to read another's need is the essence of love and the capacity to feel anxious in reaction to another's anxiety, worried when another worries, depressed with another's depression is the true proof of caring. "When another is no longer frightened by my fears, hooked by my anger, taken down with my depression, then I have reason to fear that love is waning." In such relationships of mind reading, each person maintains a radar to monitor the other and search out anxiety blips on an emotional screen; and the ability to trigger a parallel anxiety or to sympathetically sense and spontaneously share the other's fear is seen as the one true devotion.

Reading another's mind is a power play, a guilt ploy, a safety plan. It is not love.

Mind reading is trespassing. The invasion of the other's boundaries violates integrity, usurps responsibility, intrudes on and surrenders the freedom to act as an agent of personal choice.

To illustrate from the wide spectrum of mind-reading styles, consider the following fragments of conversations:

"You don't mean that. I know you better than to believe that. What you really meant was . . ."

"What you were trying to say is . . ."

"You make me so angry when you criticize me just to make me feel inferior and you better."

"He put me down because he's jealous. I know, I can read him like a book."

The attempt to read another's mind, motive or meanings without respect for the integrity of his or her own clear statement or declared intentions is vain. To steal in to discover your intent without respect for your right to think your own thoughts and choose your own words is deceit. To claim insight into your mind is to seize power to define what belongs only to another. To judge and impugn the motives of another is to induce guilt or prompt shame. To seek to predict in self-fulfilling prophecy may be a ploy to preserve safety or prove one's accuracy in pointing out the other's inadequacy. These only begin the cataloging of complications created by the bypassing of communication in "suspecting" the other's real stance

IV. Equal Integrity

I will not mind read your
thoughts

and choose my words

out of my expectations
of what I think you think.
I will feel freely
and speak frankly
what I see, I think,
I feel, I want.

(I have this fantasy
that I know your thoughts;
I have this illusion
that I can sense your feelings;
I have this conviction
that I can read your mind;

I have this delusion
that I know your real
motives.

All are wrong.
I have only hunches
that nudge me to listen.
You alone can know your
own heart.

I will speak to the you you
disclose,

not to the you I intuit.
Surprise me.)

I will not second-guess your
wants
and anticipate your
responses
to limit your right,
or inhibit your freedom
to speak frankly
or choose freely
what you see, or think,
or feel, or want.

(I have this impulse
to sense your wishes
before you express them,

to answer your questions
before you ask them,
to defend against your criticism
before you offer it,

to know you as I know
myself
so that I will be safe.
I will own this impulse
as an invitation to listen.

You alone can share your
heart.

I will look in through your
words
to see your soul.
Surprise me.)

and "inspecting" the soul within.

I will not mind read your thoughts in the endless and useless spiral of I-think-you-think-that-I-think-so-I-will-say-what-I-must-say-to-get-you-to-say-what-I-want-you-to-say. The cycle proceeds ad infinitum, ad nauseum.

When I am obsessed with what you think of me, I am no longer listening to you, I am listening to my fantasies. I am not open to you. I have already shut you out in preference to what I hope to evoke. I am not seeing you exist as another person. I am making you my mirror, my reflection of my intentions.

I want to feel freely and speak frankly. I will await the surprise of your response. I have heard what I have to say. You are the unknown in this moment. I want to hear you with open ears, open heart, open mind. I want to listen with an integrity that honors your equal integrity.

V. Equal Responsibility

"I said what I did because of your comment, and now you're interpreting it as if I were responsible for the thought; but you brought it out of me, you asked for it."

If the preceding sentence makes sad sense to you, then the snarled webs of confused responsibilities that emerge from subtle shaming or defensive blaming are no stranger to you. They are not unknown to most humans. From Adam's first circuitous avoidance of responsibility ("The woman which *you* gave me did listen to the tempter and then seduced me to taste and so did I take and eat.") to the most sophisticated strategy for shifting the onus from self to the available other, such blame and shame characterize human communication.

Little change and even less growth are possible until one owns the part of the communication process which he or she possesses. I am responsible only for my side of our dialogue. When at last I claim no more than is within my power—my own position toward you—or claim no less than what is mine—my full position toward you—then repentance, change and growth begin.

I am fully responsible for how I see things and how I say things. The perceptions I am willing to see, the thoughts I allow myself to think, the emotions I then feel, the words I speak, the intentions I will, the actions I take are all mine. Yours are yours. As I assume responsibility for my own and assume nothing of yours, I begin to act toward you with the simplicity, the honesty and the integrity of one who is being accountable for his or her own stance and respectful of the stance of the neighbor. Accepting responsibility for the self ends punitive cycles and invites us to move linearly, ends vertical attacks and evokes our communicating horizontally.

I am responsible—this is good news—for whatever I do. I am response-able—this is hopeful news—for whatever I choose. I want to act in appreciation of our equal responsibility.

VI. Equal Conciliation

"What can I do to unsay what I have said, undo what I have done? Perhaps I could show you how sorry I am by putting myself down in 'apology'; it might even inspire you to put yourself down in return or to invite me up in restoring the relationship."

Vertical moves are means for manipulating the other's sympathy, guilt, anger, revenge, or sense of injustice, injury or indignity. Some regress all

V. Equal Responsibility

I will take
full responsibility
for how I see things
and how I say things.
I will neither
blame you for my responses

nor accept blame for yours.
I am always responsible.
I am never to blame.

(The words I speak,
the emotions I feel,
the thoughts I think,
the actions I take
are mine; for them
I am fully responsible.)

I will honor
your sole responsibility
for how you see things
and how you say things.
I will neither
accept   shame   for   my
responses
nor shame you for yours.
You are always accountable,
you need never feel shame.

(The words you speak,
the emotions you feel,
the thoughts you think,
the actions you take
are yours and for them
I am in no way responsible.)

the way back to threat (I've apologized for my part, what's stopping you?) or to bargaining (I'll grovel nicely if you'll come to meet me acceptingly) or to manipulation (I act one down so you will feel uncomfortable above me and come down one step too. Then we both can move back up, etc., etc.).

Horizontal conciliation takes place in the levels of persuasion and dialogue. I can affirm my sadness for the specific behavior, reaffirm my intentions to act toward you in new ways that are more just and fair, and confirm my promise to be trustworthy in the future. All these are level, frank requests which offer persuasive evidence that I am taking full responsibility for my part in any injury between us and responding fully to make appropriate steps toward setting it right.

Equal conciliation takes a series of steps: (1) owning my words and acts; (2) seeing them as the results of my decisions (they are my choices, and not determined by the situation, the circumstances, the other parties); (3) prizing them as my responses (they were the best I was able to see in that moment or I would have chosen otherwise. I now see more clearly a better way); (4) recognizing where they are hurtful (they were not conducive to creative relating); (5) modifying them willingly (there is no need to defend, to pretend that it was good, to persist in what was not useful. I will change); (6) seeking a mutually satisfying relationship (so that right relationships are either restored or newly achieved).

All of these are level steps of equal regard, taken in openness to equal conciliation while assuming full responsibility for the portion of the interaction which is mine and attempting no manipulation of the part that belongs to the other party.

VII. Equal Wholeness

The goal is communion between intimates, community between associates, communion and community that are a continuing invitation to wholeness as persons, and increasing health in the community that connects and directs our lives together.

In dialogue, I strive toward greater presence and authenticity with you. I want in no way to squander the privilege of being fully the self I am now as I am with you. I equally welcome your being fully present and genuine with me. I want in no way to hamper your freedom to be all that you are as you are with me.

What if, in being with each other, we become such a mutual, equal invitation to life? Then we will have touched center to center, and deepened the meaning of our lives together.

Once a day, minimum, I need to give a "whole message," a signal communicating all of myself to some person who is significant to me.

So much of my life talk is simple information, data, facts. If I let that become my total output for a whole day I lose something very precious, very important to me—sensitive human contact. To make contact with my whole self requires an investment of not only words, but a gift of feelings, an expression of my deepest insides. Feeling as deeply about life as I do I need to stay in union with my depths lest they become separated from my surface, and I become superficial. So once a day I want to sound the depths, reaching down, down and let the message of the still, cool ocean floor of the soul speak to another.

At times when I drop the plumb line of awareness, I find turbulence along my inner ocean floor. Confused churnings and riled sediments stir up

VI. Equal Conciliation

I will own
my words and acts,
see them as my choices,
prize   them   as   my
responses,
recognize where they are
hurtful,
modify them willingly
to seek a mutually
satisfying
relationship.

(When hurts occur

and we are distant
I will own my part
of our two-person problem,

examine my words and acts
as my part of our relationship.

I will admit my regretting
and repenting,
and choose new ways of
being with you.)

I will admit
my mistakes.
I will not grovel

to gain your approval

nor ask you to "apologize"
to earn my acceptance.
I will change my part
in our two-person
problem.

(When   there   is   pain
between us,
and we are alienated,
I will not lay the problem
at your doorstep, demand-
ing "apology."
Nor claim the problem

as my sole property, offering "apology."

I will see it as between us

and work through until we
break through.)

waves of painful feelings. To talk of this uncertainty allows the waves of emotion to ripple up to the surface and re-order a part of my life. I need a sensitive conversation to truly own and express such depths. When I am willingly open to another I can be more genuinely open to the inner wisdom which arises from a whirlpool where two great currents clash face to face.

At times the depths stir with joy and a profound sense of well-being generates a mellow richness and warmth. To share this with another can bring tears of joy. The temperatures of the deeps may also rise in anger and the molten core of personhood may push out intrusions of inner rage. To own this, to affirm it, and to express its wisdom in constructive ways releases power.

When a message exchanged with another is an expression of the entire self, a deep sense of well-being is shared for the moment by two persons. If the other is not free to reciprocate at the moment, a portion of the richness is lost, but the significance of the moment for the initiator is diminished but not lost. Contact has been made. The fact that it is not completely mutual is sad, but that sadness is present to some degree in most human interchange. Each of us reaches out with more than another is able to perceive. "We know in part, we long for the moment when we will be known and be able to know without interference" (see 1 Cor. 13:12).

Contact, when two persons meet core-to-core, nourishes life, identifies meaning, excites growth, and bids both self and other to live. I need it daily if I am truly alive. Such contact frees friendship to

VII. Equal Wholeness

I want in no way
to squander my freedom
to be fully me
when I am with you.

(What if, in being with you,
I am more eager for life,
I am more in touch with
feelings,

I am more sensitive to
myself,

I am more reverent toward
you,

I am more open toward others,

I am more responsible with
values,

I am more alive toward God,
I am more aware of what
endures?

Then we have truly met,

and we enrich each other.)

I want in no way
to hamper your freedom
to be wholly you
when you are with me.

(What if, in being with me,
you are more excited by life,

you are more rich in feelings,

you are more tender with
yourself,

you are more gentle toward
me,

you are more acceptant of
others,

you are more committed to
values,
you are more aware of God,

you are more shaped by
what is eternal?
Then we have truly
touched,
and we deepen each other.)

be a dialogue of reverent awe. Such contact frees marriage to be totally intimate while honoring the distinct uniqueness of each. Such contact frees counseling to be an encounter of profound worship of the Creator of unique persons. Such contact frees prayer to be an intimate relationship of silent communion.

For Exploration in the Bible

The goal of mutuality in loving respect is a central thread in biblical values and teaching for living. Trace this central theme through the following passages.

Leviticus 19:15-18: "You shall love your neighbor as yourself, for I am Yahweh" (see v. 18). In matters of justice, of gossip, of acting as a witness, of dealing with hatred, with wrongdoing, with anger, the central principle is equal loving regard.

Matthew 19:19; 22:39; Mark 12:31; Luke 10:27: Jesus calls us to equal loving regard as the central motivation for our human relationships. In resolution of conflicts in living, in respect for the worth of others, in fulfilling God's highest intentions for us, we show our profound love for God by the way we love our neighbor as ourselves.

John 13:34,35; 15:9-14: In caring for others as persons of equal preciousness we do not draw lines to easily define how far love will go. Jesus did not draw back from acting by unconditional love but "even unto death." His model for action was God, who draws no lines (see Matt. 5:43-48). Thus loving in equal, mutual regard is a commitment to a caring style of life without the reservations of imposed conditions of worth.

Romans 13:9; Galatians 5:14; Ephesians 5:28,29; James 2:8. In the letters of Paul, the prin-

Communication As Dialogue

I will claim my right
to be equally heard.
I am I.
I want to be heard.

I
Equal
Hearing

I will respect your
right
to be equally heard.
You are you.
I want to hear you.

I will claim my full
ownership
for my side of the dia-
logue.
I will speak for myself.
I will not let you
speak for me.

II
Equal
Ownership

I will respect your sole
ownership
for your side of the
dialogue.
You will speak for
yourself.
I will not speak for
you.

I will meet you now
as the person you
truly are.
I will stop myself
from speaking
to my image of you.
I cancel the demand
that you be what you
were
or become what I
want.

III
Equal
Presence

I will be with you now
as the person I truly
am.
I will not be trying
to match or fulfill
your image of me.
I claim the freedom
to change what I was
and choose who I am
becoming.

I will honor your
boundaries and
not mind read your
thoughts
to choose my words
out of my expecta-
tions
of what I think you
think.
I will feel frankly and
speak frankly
what I see, I think, I
feel, I want.

IV
Equal
Integrity

I will respect your
intentions
and not second-guess
your wants
or anticipate your
responses
to limit your right
or inhibit your free-
dom
to speak and choose
what you see, think,
feel, want.

**V
Equal
Responsibility**

I take full responsibility
for how I see things
and how I say things.
I will neither blame
you
for my responses
nor accept blame for
yours.
I am always responsible.
I am never to blame.

I honor your sole
responsibility
for how you see
things
and how you say
things.
I will accept no shaming
for my responses
nor shame you for
yours.
You are always
accountable.
You need never feel
shame.

**VI
Equal
Conciliation**

I will own my words
and acts,
see them as my
choices,
prize them as my
responses,
recognize where they
are hurtful,
discuss them openly
and
modify them willingly
to seek a mutually
satisfying relationship.

I will admit my mistakes.
I will not grovel
to gain your approval
nor ask you to "apologize"
to earn my acceptance.
You may speak your
part,
I will deal with my
part
in our two-person
problem.

**VII
Equal
Freedom**

I want in no way
to squander my freedom
to be fully me
when I am with you.

I want in no way
to hamper your freedom
to be wholly you
when you are with
me.

ciple of caring in equal mutual respect is taught as the central basis for living justly and serving joyfully. Equal regard (agape love) values others as equal in importance, in worth, in preciousness as persons.

This mutuality shapes each area of our ethical decisions and our moral responsibility. Issues of fairness are defined by concern for equal regard. Communication with each other moves toward equal dialogue. Sharing of power is done in mutual concern. Choices on how to relate to each other are guided by mutual caring for the good of each.

For Personal Growth

These items provide a way of reflecting on personal dialogue skills. Check the most accurate rating possible for your practice of each.

Definitely *Probably* *Neutral* *Unlikely* *Never*

1. I often defer to another and listen on and on without asking for equal time to share. — — — — —

2. I sometimes share my thoughts, feelings and experiences at length without pausing to wait or ask for the other's view from the other side. — — — — —

3. I don't mind when someone who knows me well speaks for us both or assumes our agreement. — — — — —

4. I frequently feel I understand the other well enough to be able to answer for us on a request that includes

both of us. _ _ _ _ _

5. I trust my picture of who you are to represent your preferences quite accurately. _ _ _ _ _

6. I want to live up to the expectations and hopes that I sense others have for me. _ _ _ _ _

7. I often read people by their unintentional signals even though their words say the reverse. _ _ _ _ _

8. I have little difficulty in figuring out what people are thinking or how they are reacting to me. _ _ _ _ _

9. I find that others can get to me and make me angry or depressed no matter what I try. _ _ _ _ _

10. I feel responsible when someone important to me is angry at me. _ _ _ _ _

11. I do not feel satisfied after another has hurt me until I hear a real apology. _ _ _ _ _

12. I sometimes eat my words and feel bad about myself for having said just what I thought and felt. _ _ _ _ _

13. I have discovered that too much openness and too much honesty cause real trouble, so I work for tact and diplomacy. _ _ _ _ _

14. I do not think that friend-

ship gives anyone the right
to burden others with negative feelings that are better
forgotten.   — — — — —

If your check marks fell to the left of the center
column then you have come to accept or support
more monologue than dialogue. If to the right you
are working toward equal dialogue.

For Dyadic or Group Process

1. Discussion of levels of contact. Reflect on
the amount of communication you offer in each
level from threat to dialogue when in conversation
with (a) a misbehaving child, (b) an employee, (c) a
friend, (d) a clerk in a store, (e) a spouse, (f) a son
or daughter, (g) a parent, (h) _____ .
At which level do you characteristically begin?
Where do you prefer ending? Where do you more
often end?

2. Role play the five levels. If possible, each person select a level that was used in a recent interchange with another, whether a conflictual or a
complementary interaction. Play the response as it
was. Discuss. Then play the scene as you would
have liked to respond as you see it now in hindsight.

3. Pair in dyads. Take the covenant entitled
"Communication As Dialogue" as the basis for
reexamining your friendship, colleague, or marital
contract for communicating. Renegotiate each of
these seven areas to move toward more open, effective and mutual dialogue. If this is done as a
group, return to the circle and share the two areas
of greatest excitement for growth. (Each speaking
for the self, of course.)

How can we be pals
    when you speak English
    and I speak English
    and you never understand me
    and I never understand you?
Carl Sandburg

For communication to have meaning
it must have a life.
It must transcend "you and me" and become "us."
If I truly communicate, I see in you
a life that is not me and partake of it.
And you see and partake of me.
In a small way we then grow out of our old selves
and become something new.
To have this kind of sharing
I cannot enter a conversation clutching myself.
I must enter it with loose boundaries.
I must give myself to the relationship,
and be willing to be what grows out of it.
Hugh Prather[e]

4 ■ Leveling

"I want equality; I will hear you equally."

When in stress, some people immediately talk down to the person seen as a wrongdoer. Their mouths turn down. The words are downers. The opponent is put down.

In contrast, others instinctively talk up in response to any threat. Their mouths turn up in fixed smiles. The words are aimed upward since they feel instantly down in any stress.

When in distress do you talk *up* to the other? Or talk *down*? Or talk *with*?

Vertical communications—"talking up" or "talking down"—are often characteristic of oldest children, youngest children, only children who have little experience in talking with siblings as peers, with others as equals, with intimates in horizontal relationships. An oldest child, for example, often is turned into a parental assistant and communicates quite well when talking up to elders or down to juniors, but has little skill at leveling with others. As tension rises or threat surprises the vertical communicator, the words rise or fall in response.

Talking down has many forms: blaming ("What I want to know is whose fault is it?"); scolding ("Why did you do such a stupid thing?"); judging

("That was a wrong move"); belittling ("How many times do I have to tell you . . ."); instructing ("I can tell you how to do it better"); supervising ("Here, let me show you how"); to begin a long, long list you should already know by now (Hear me talking down? I'm a youngest son.).

Talking up is equally diverse and rich: placating ("It's all my fault. How can I repay you?"); apologizing ("I'm so sorry I blew it again"); groveling ("How could I have done such a stupid thing?"); ingratiating ("I'll make it up to you somehow"); yielding ("Yes, yes, I'll gladly do anything you say"). Please understand me, I'm sorry I can't be more explicit (There I go talking up again, I grew up on the bottom.).

Vertical communications—words that come down hard on another or lines that seek to play up to the other—are seldom effective communications since they are not ways to commune. Their function is to coerce (Down, bad boy!) or seduce (Let me up, I'm a good boy!).

Horizontal communication—talking with—is the open exchange of ideas, information, feelings and requests that takes place between persons who recognize each other as equals. Such leveling is equally free to give and to receive, to speak and to hear, to confirm another's equal worth, to be affirmed by the other. It is truly a *co*-munication rather than a *uni*-cation exchanged in a vertical altercation.

Value judgments are the most common vertical comments. The ever-present human tendency to evaluate virtually everything from whether one likes the weather to how one judges his or her peers constantly clouds attempts at communicating. Momentarily, one's eyes snap shut when a criticism is received. This involuntary response is so fast with most people that it must be videotaped and rerun in slow motion for it to be seen clearly. But it's there. At the sound of a discouraging word, the first defense is to shut it out. A pause follows, then the conversation begins again, but proceeds with caution. The pause is so brief with many persons that it must be recorded and replayed at slower speed to be heard sharply. But it's there. The cut of critical words stalls thought or stuns the thinker when dropped on the person from above.

Values affirmed without an attempt at imposing them on another can flow in open and free exchange. If I am appreciating my freely chosen values and equally appreciating your freedom to choose yours, we can level with each other from highly contrasting world views and worlds of values without either of us coming down on the other. Since lasting values are formed slowly, chosen voluntarily and held firmly deep within one's solid self, then we offer most to each other when we speak center to center, core to core, solid self to solid self. Then values can call to values and basic beliefs speak to basal beliefs.

So—why on earth should you talk down to others in pseudosuperiority? Who do you think you are, laying your demands on others from above? Sin is any choice to live over another in dominance. Sin is any ploy used to play God. (Reread this paragraph. Note what you are feeling in response to a "why," a "should," and the other downers I slipped in, no matter how true they may be.)

Sorry about that. Who am I to come down on you, dear reader whom I cannot see, whose readership I have just lost. Dear editor, since you are the only one who will ever finish reading this book,

Talking Down

Blaming
Scolding
Judging
Belittling
Instructing
Supervising

Equal
give
and
take

**Talking
With**

Mutual
hearing
and
being heard

Yielding
Ingratiating
Groveling
Apologizing
Placating

Talking Up

Diagram 10

please overlook my getting carried away. (There I go, apologizing, placating, talking up again. Sin is also any choice to live under you in submissive dependence, making you my god, my guru, my idol. And nothing loses hearers, readers, or friends like talking up.)

We are of equal worth. We each deserve the privilege of equal words. We can stand with each other, with the freedom to think, feel and speak, horizontally, equally, levelly.

Leveling—Step One: Suspend Judgment

"The place for peacemakers is the armed forces," a student in my class insists. "As a chaplain, I minister to those who keep the world safe."

His view of peacemaking is directly opposite to mine. How can we hear each other when we face in such different directions? I agree with so much of this man's basic values and perspectives, yet I disagree with the central commitment that shapes his life project. Is it possible to really hear his concerns when I differ so sharply?

"A person's worth is shown in his or her performance. It's the only measure we have," a colleague reports. "Worth, performance, produce— they're all one ball of wax."

His way of valuing people is the reverse of mine. How can I hear his concern when I am so opposed to his values? Can I offer genuine respect for how he cares for others even though I think it does not go far enough?

Believing in another who believes what is to me unbelievable, respecting another who accepts what is to me unacceptable, truly hearing another who holds the unheard of, demands special listening skills, skills that enable one to hear the person while placing the particular views on hold.

If I choose to hear you in spite of differences and disagreements, I must learn the art of suspending judgment while continuing open hearing, caring, and mutual regard.

For example: I can't believe what you are saying. My truth lies in the opposite direction. Believing it as I do suggests that your truth lies. How can I hear you accurately when I think you are so wrong? How can I fairly compare your truth with my truth and use both to find a firmer truth? The secret of empathic listening without immediate judgment is "bracketing."

[Although I thoroughly disagree with what you just said] I will listen to hear how you arrived at your point of view and to discover what is so attractive to you in that way of thinking. [If I bracket my judgment] I will not lose my concern, nor will I use it to filter yours.

[Although I stand on different premises and am proceeding in the opposite direction] I want to hear how the world appears from your vantage point and come to appreciate you and your view without necessarily joining you in it.

[I bracket my beliefs, for the moment.] I seek to understand yours. [I suspend my judgments, temporarily.] I follow you in your direction of thought. When I can articulate your point of view clearly, then I will be able to clearly share mine. Bracketing my own perspective clears my channels so you can enter and be recognized; it holds my convictions in abeyance to allow yours free admittance. Having entertained and examined your ideas, I can more accurately compare, contrast and in some areas combine my concerns with yours.

To bracket is to respect. Your perspective is one part of your world of thought, and I refuse to see the part as the whole. You are not just a material-

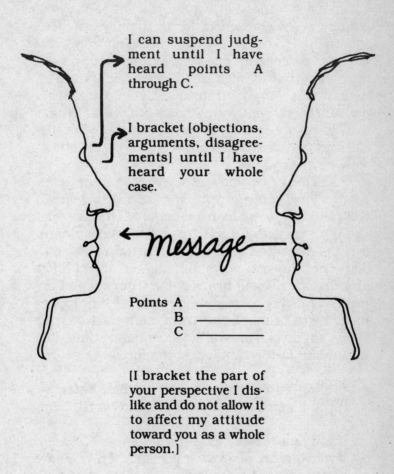

I can suspend judgment until I have heard points A through C.

I bracket [objections, arguments, disagreements] until I have heard your whole case.

Message

Points A _____
       B ========
       C _____

[I bracket the part of your perspective I dislike and do not allow it to affect my attitude toward you as a whole person.]

Diagram 11

ist, a militarist, a humanist, a nationalist or any other "ist." Nor am I just a personalist, a pacifist, a theist, a universalist. You are more than any one point of view; indeed, you are more than all your points of view combined, for in the next moment you are free to redirect, correct, extend, transcend any past perspective and choose another. So I will bracket, intentionally, my disagreements until I have heard you. I will bracket your individual point of view from your total world view. Thus I can affirm, appreciate, accept you as you while disconfirming, discussing, disagreeing with one of your views or values.

I will not see you as a wrong person even though I will confront your view as a wrong view. I will not judge you as an inadequate thinker even though I may argue that your explanation of an event is not adequate. I will not put you down as a sister or a brother while putting out how I differ and disagree. I will bracket me from each of my views. Thus I can examine it, improve it or repent of it. I will bracket you from each part of your vision so you can be heard, valued, and stimulated by our similarities and our differences.

Leveling—Step Two: Disconnect Self-Esteem

If you listen to me, then I must be worth hearing.

If you ignore me, I must be a bore.

If you approve of my views or values, then I have something of worth to offer.

If you disapprove of my comment or contribution, then I apparently had nothing to say.

If I cannot be with you without using your comments for self-evaluation, then leveling will be impossible. If I am preoccupied with what you think of me, then I have already shut you out. I am looking at the reflection of me I am reading from your responses. I am making you my mirror. When I am looking for reflected esteem I do not see you as a person with your own existence. I only see the interest in your eye, hear the approval in your voice, read esteem in your smile. Or missing these, I see only rejection or disapproval.

When I make success in any particular conflict a measure of my self-worth, I am much more likely to become over-involved, oversensitive, or easily angry.

Connecting self-esteem to the moment's interpersonal success makes open, level communication difficult and often impossible. When self-esteem is threatened, defensiveness rises and listening is sharply reduced.

This connection between self-esteem and performance is a false one. It is often made by parents in the hope that it will produce motivation, discipline and self-control in the child. It boomerangs.

When one feels good about a success, it does not follow that he or she will automatically feel good about the self. Self-esteem and performance-esteem are two separate valuations. When they are disconnected, one can feel bad about the performance of the moment without making an enduring judgment about the self. Temporary judgments can look at a particular behavior as effective or ineffective, as good or bad, as meeting or falling short of one's goals. Enduring judgments about the self become independent of external valuations when one recognizes that worth is not achieved, it is a given to be claimed and celebrated.

The connection between person and performance is rooted in the basic ways we learn to think. When another disagrees with a thought we have expressed, we take it personally. He disagrees with me, we say. When another criticizes our performance, we take it as a personal reference. He didn't like me, we conclude. We have identified the two different referents into one. Thought and thinker are seen as one and the same.

Disconnecting this false connection frees one to see the self as person, rather than the performance or product.

I am the thinker, not the thought. If the thought is criticized or I am confronted, I am free to correct it in the next thought.

I am the agent, not the decision. I can choose again as I learn from the consequences of the previous choice.

I am the doer, not the deed. I am free to change and to grow.

When in conversation, I want to be able to accept the other's perspective as a contrast and a contribution to my vision of reality, not a commentary on me.

When in controversy, I want to be able to hear the other's disagreement with my position for what it is, a disagreement with a point of view, not a rejection of me.

When in dialogue, I want to accept the other's feedback as a complementary or a counter conviction, not as a critique of me.

Leveling—Step Three: Define Yourself

Note the difference in feeling, tone, content, impact between the following comments:

"We should be much more cooperative so things wouldn't get so tense around here."

"You get the feeling that no one wants to cooperate with anybody else around here."

"They say that a staff's productivity is directly related to their ability to work cooperatively."

"It's a real source of frustration to everyone when cooperation is as low as it has been recently."

"I'm not happy with the level of cooperation on the staff; I'm willing to put in some extra time to work on it with each other."

Note how the speaker avoids taking a position in all but the last. "We" language is usually pretentious. Pretending to speak for others it actually speaks for no one in attempting to speak for everyone. "You" language is hopelessly undefined. It purports to speak for the other, or an impersonal "you" speaks for anyone. "They" language appeals to authorities, experts, enemies, any available jury. "It" language places responsibility on "it" whatever "it" may be.

"I" language is responsible, honest, humble and immediate. "I" language risks taking a position. "I" language allows clear expression of feelings, direct declaration of views, firm affirmation of values. "I" language reflects the speaker's choice of an *I* position, a self-defined identity of inner-directed choice.

In taking an *I* position I become a responder, not a reactor. In responding, I am a free agent; in reacting, I am the victim of my environment. In responding, I define what I am willing to do in any relationship; I claim responsibility for my own thoughts, feelings, words and actions. In reacting, I feel myself pressured by the situation, oppressed by circumstances, shaped by the external realities around me.

A *you* relationship refuses to risk defining the self by focusing on the other in blaming, accusing, analyzing, diagnosing, treating, trying to help, trying to change the other. Responsibility for the self and for the other are mixed and confused.

I Position	We-You-They-It Position
I am a *responder*.	I am a *reactor*.
I respond to the other's pain or joy freely.	I react to the other's pain or joy automatically.

I can respond saying—
    I am . . .
    I think . . .
    I feel . . .
    I want . . .
	I must react saying—
	    You make me feel . . .
	    You make me do . . .
	    You won't let me . . .
	    You keep me from . . .

I will be radically honest—
    "I don't like what is now happening between us. I am willing to take this step to change it. I want to hear your response."
	I have to be critically frank—
	    "You are driving me up a wall, you are making me very angry, you must change or you are ruining our relationship."

Each of us is sole owner of his or her feelings, choices and actions and is free to respond in love.	Each must feel for the other, hurt for the other, protect the other; so each must react in obligation.

An *I* relationship accepts the obvious fact that self and other are polar parts of any relation or any transaction, and owns the self's part in the two-(or more) person problem. The focus is on changing my stance toward the situation, my response to the tension into a clear *I* position.

In an *I* position, one speaks for the self, from the self, inviting the same from others. Having discovered that none of us can rightfully speak for another except upon request, one who takes an *I* position opts for the simplicity of personal, confessional speech. This simplifies relationships with others by taking what may seem like a superficial step, but turns out to be a profound change.

"I" language offers the most clarity to confusing communications, the most presence and intimacy to encounters, the most power in working through conflict.

"I" language narrows the contribution down to the only accurate assessment one party can offer to a confusing conversation—how I see it, how I evaluate it, what I want to do now. An astounding percentage of the comments made in any conflict are *we-you-they-it* statements. When one person chooses to use *I* messages, blaming, manipulation, criticizing are sharply decreased.

"I" language invites genuineness and intimacy. When I can report candidly what I feel, think, want of another, I feel immediately closer to the other. When another responds from a clear *I* position, I feel more close, more understanding, more equal.

Define yourself in communication. Give up attempting to define the other person's part in the interaction, altercation or relationship. Define your own stance. Respect the other person's right to take his own position or to decide on her own

You Messages	I Messages
"You're not listening, you're a thousand miles away. What's wrong with you today?"	"I'm lonely, I'd like to talk."
"You make me so angry."	"I am angry that you are late."
"You know so much about everything, don't you?"	"I resent hearing answers when I don't even think there's a problem."
"You've monopolized the time, you don't let anyone get a word in edgeways."	"I grow tired and resentful when you run on and on; I'd like equal time."
"You really are terrific, you have the greatest sense of humor."	"I really like your sense of humor. I enjoy you so much."

Hidden You Messages

"I feel that you never hear a word I say."	(Note that this is (a) not a feeling, but a judgment, (b) really a *you* message in concealment.)
"I'm beginning to think that you don't care about how I see things at all."	(Note that this is (a) mind-reading of the other's motivations and (b) a hidden *you* message.)

part in the relationship. Speak for yourself.

Leveling—Step Four: Discard Questions

"Don't you think that . . .?" (No, I don't think that. You do. And you're asking me a leading question to induce or seduce agreement.)

"Why did you do that . . .?" (I have no good reason. Perhaps that's the point of the question, to punish, shame or embarrass me, to show that I have no good reason.)

"When are you going to do something about . . .?" (This is not really a question; it's a demand, but it is concealed within an innocuous sounding request for information.)

"If you were in charge of this operation, wouldn't you rather have . . .?" (This is a hypothetical question whose real function is to slip in a criticism without taking the responsibility for it.)

"What did you mean by that?" (This is a multiple choice question. It might mean (a) tell me once again, (b) was that meant to be a dig? (c) how could you say that to me? (d) why do you always beat around the bush? (e) none, all, several of the above.)

"Are you bragging or complaining?" (Neither. This is not a question; it's an either/or trap. By setting up the only two alternatives possible— answer yes or no—all other options have been eliminated.)

"Didn't you promise to . . .?" (This is a setup. It maneuvers the listener into a compromising or contradictory position. Once in the corner, the victim is ready for the hatchet.)

Questions are much too treacherous to use when tensions are high. They are not too trustworthy when all is well. When in doubt, use statements. As a simple rule, to communicate a message, make a statement; to gather information, use a question. If what I really intend is to make a statement, then I want to do it openly, forthrightly, frankly in a clear statement. If what I desire is further information, I will be free to ask a question. Even then I will be aware that the question will be less effective than a simple statement reporting what I want to know, or a simple invitation to go further, clarify, explain, disclose.

When I am plied with questions I will not answer questions with questions. I will move to as simple statements as possible. Simplicity is to state what is best stated, ask what is appropriate to ask, and refuse to confuse the two.

When I listen, I want to reply with the simplest, clearest words possible. I want my responses to be a constant invitation for others to share more freely, see more clearly, own their experience more fully and feel more alive, in touch with their real feelings, aware of their own insight.

Leveling—Step Five: Reply Simply

"Isn't that interesting," a friend of mine used to say. He said it when he agreed, when he disagreed, when confused, when threatened, even when bored. He had developed a standard reply for all listening situations. It expressed interest without expressing interest.

The art of giving a simple, level, and inviting reply frees another to continue or to explore more deeply. The following spectrum of responses moves from one-word replies to complete rephrasing of the other's words.

1. Repeat. A very short reply that simply repeats the key word, the feeling word, the puzzling word.

"I haven't been doing much of anything this

Discard Questions

The most frequently misused communication pattern is the question. Questions can be clever, coercive, concealed ways of offering multilevel messages, hidden pressures, or innocent manipulation.

Questions lead

"Isn't it true that . . ."
"Wouldn't you rather . . ."

Statements inform

"I believe that . . ."
"I would rather . . ."

Questions punish

"Why did you say that?"
"What's wrong with you?"

Statements report

"I don't like what you . . ."
"I'm unhappy with . . ."

Questions seduce

"If you were in charge of this, wouldn't you have . . ."

Statements invite

"I would like . . ."
"I would prefer . . ."

Questions command

"When are you going to . . ."
"Why don't you get to . . ."

Statements demand

"I want change."
"I want cooperation."

Questions deceive

"Why don't you choose . . ."
"What did you mean by that?"

Statements disclose

"I'm happy for you to choose."
"I don't understand . . ."

Questions divide

"Are you bragging or complaining?"
"Do you agree with them or me?"

Statements unite

"I'd like to hear how you feel about it."
"I want to know your view."

Questions bind

"Isn't it true that you once . . ."
"Didn't you promise to . . ."

Statements free

"I'd like to talk about . . ."
"I'm still wanting what we . . ."

past week, I guess I just feel too lousy these days."

"Lousy?"

"Yes, ever since I got laid off I just . . ."

Some of the best responses in listening are short, pithy and contain a request to keep talking. The eloquent and encouraging sounds of "uh-huh," "oh," or "mmm . . ." often say more than words. They are feeling sounds, empathy sounds. When used sparingly, fittingly, genuinely, they say "tell me more," they communicate understanding without saying the arbitrary "I understand," "I see," "I know how you feel." When these are said, the listener more often than not doubts the claim and is not sure he or she is understood, seen, or "felt with."

2. Reflect. A short reflection of what is heard as a key phrase or feeling can invite further exploration. Rather than parroting the same words, the intent is to make a mutually interchangeable response so that what the listener says in her words could be accepted by the speaker as what he intended to say.

"I get so frustrated with my job that I want to quit, yet it's the best job I've ever had."

"You both love and hate your job."

"I sure do!"

3. Request. A simple request can invite further conversation without stopping the stream of thought. The request functions as an invitation to go farther, perhaps deeper, often narrower in a more focused direction.

"Say more." "Push that out a little further." "Tell about the feelings you've been having." "Yes, I'd like to hear what happened."

4. Understanding. A clear affirmation of the wish to understand and an "active-listening" report of what was said in one's own words can often facilitate sharing. Care must be taken to not add interpretation unless that is your intent and is openly admitted, as we'll describe later.

"I get so fed up with my mom's cross-examinations. She can ask so many questions about stuff that doesn't matter. I get so mad. I'm really glad she's interested in my schoolwork but I feel like a kid being supervised."

"I want to understand this. You really do like it that she's interested in you, but you also wish she'd show it by listening to how you want to say it rather than asking all of her questions."

5. *Support*. When one is risking the sharing of scary emotions, or revealing parts of the self that are uncomfortable as they are put in words, a word of support can free the other to go on to feel his feelings and face her real thoughts.

"I know I shouldn't feel this way, but sometimes I really resent it that she got the farm."

"Resentment sounds like a natural feeling to me."

. "I guess it is, if I could just talk with her about it."

"I bet you could."

6. *Interpretive*. Whether done briefly or at full length, offering an alternate interpretation of events can free the speaker to look at the circumstances in a new light and perhaps claim greater responsibility. This may be as simple as relabeling (you referred to him as "obstinate," try thinking of him as "firm") or it may be a full reframing of the point of view. (You are judging yourself as a failure since your 13-year-old son is preferring his dad. That sounds like successful mothering to me. You are nudging him toward the model he needs as he is becoming a man.) Often it is just a step of clarifying what seems obvious in the tone of voice but

is denied by the words.

"I feel so— well— *concerned* that she would act like that."

"Concerned— and upset, and a little angry too perhaps?"

"No— well, yes, *yes* I am."

In all responses, the word choice is the smallest part of the message. Some researchers go so far as to mark its emotional impact as only seven percent. Tone of voice is 38 percent, facial expressions, posture and gestures form a full 58 percent. We learn early to read the person first and decipher the words second. As we age we sometimes learn to ignore the body language or the intonation and stick with just the facts of the words themselves. Tuning out the tone is missing the major part of the message. Hearing the whole person with childlike simplicity and adult responsivity can help us regain presence and immediacy with each other.

To help bring tone of voice and intent of heart together, stay level. Suspend judgment, disconnect self-esteem, define yourself rather than the other, discard questions, reply simply. This is choosing dialogue.

Listening to the whole person is a skill to be learned. Eyes can be taught to see more clearly, ears to hear more sharply. And the reverse is equally true. We can learn to hear with our eyes and see with our ears.

Hearing with the eyes is attending to the other's face and to all he or she says in expression, facials, gestures, posture and manner. The question behind the question is seldom heard; it is more often seen in the other's movement and behavior. Often with the eye we truly hear the other. We see with the ears as listening becomes

Rules About Tones, Overtones and Undertones

1. When the tone of voice conflicts with the content of a message, the receiver will respond first to the tone.

2. When a verbal message conflicts with the nonverbal message, the receiver will act first according to the nonverbal message.
"I think people should wait until they know each other very well before they kiss," the young woman says as they say goodnight at her front door. She continues to stand looking at his shy smile. He kisses her, she responds warmly.

3. When a compliment and a criticism are offered together, the receiver will hear only the criticism.
"I like your taste in clothes, but you've put on some weight, haven't you?"

4. When two comments are connected with a "but," no one recalls what was said before the word "but."
"I enjoyed the evening with you, but when you started talking about people not present, I wished I were somewhere else."

visual. Seeing pictures as words are heard allows one to catch the vivid images that the other is seeing.

To listen for the word-windows, to look through them with attentive eyes that seek to replicate what the other is visualizing. To fantasize the pictures being drawn by the other's metaphors, similes, or suggestive words and to explore them in appreciation are often the richest ways of listening with eyes and ears.

Hearing the whole person is hearing the meaner as well as the meaning.

For Exploration in the Bible

The most profound words on suspending judgment are spoken by Jesus in the Sermon on the Mount. Consider them.

"Judge not, that you be not judged. For with the judgment you pronounce you will be judged, and the measure you give will be the measure you get. Why do you see the speck that is in your brother's eye, but do not notice the log in your own eye? Or how can you say to your brother, 'Let me take the speck

For Reflection

Suspend judgment in *humility*. (Judge only in full awareness that you will also be judged.)

Suspend judgment in *honesty*. (Judge only in full awareness that in judging you judge yourself.)

out of your eye,'
when there is the log
    in your own eye?
You hypocrite, first
    take the log
out of your own eye,
and then you will see
    clearly
to take the speck out of
    your   brother's
    eye.
(Matthew 7:1-5)

Suspend judgment
    in *integrity*.
(Judge only after tak-
    ing   action   to
    accept and apply
    your judgment to
    yourself.)

Suspend judgment
    in *love*.
(Judge only as you
    would want to be
    judged.)

"Judge not, and you
    will be be judged;
condemn not, and you
    will not be con-
    demned;
forgive, and you will be
    forgiven;
give and it will be given
    you. . . .
For the measure you
    give
will be the measure
    you get back."
(Luke 6:37,38)

Suspend judgment
    in humility,
    in honesty,
    in integrity,
    in love.

"You have no excuse,
O man, whoever you
    are,
when   you   judge
    another;

for in passing judg-
    ment upon him
you condemn yourself,
because you, the
    judge,
are doing the very
    same things."
(Romans 2:1)

For Personal Growth

The steps toward leveling can be learned, strengthened, deepened by mental rehearsal and behavioral experimentation. Review the steps and make notes on new behaviors you can test to move from vertical to level-horizontal communication.

Step One: Suspend Judgment
    Stop, Look, Listen before making any
    evaluation or evaluative comments.
    Hear, understand, value the other first.
Step Two: Disconnect Self-Esteem
    Wait, Reflect, Choose before reacting
    to any real or imagined threat.
    Then respond as a whole person instead of
    reacting in part.
Step Three: Define Your Self
    Pause, Reaffirm your own stance.
    Respond with equal regard from a
    position of equal dignity as a centered "I."
Step Four: Discard Questions
    Report what you see, think, feel, want
    in simple declarative statements that
    decrease stress by defining intentions with-
    out concealment.
Step Five: Reply Simply
    Reply simply, clearly, directly,
    non-defensively. This reduces your
    stress and distress in the other.

1. Review a recent threat situation in which you were tempted either to react vertically by coming down on the other with blaming, scolding, judging, belittling, etc., or to talk up in yielding, groveling, placating. Plan three responses that incorporate the above elements in a level, equal, mutual response. Reply for the other person with the words you could anticipate.

2. Reflect on ways in which you react vertically to your self in intrapersonal conflict. Does an inner tyrant, as in most of us, talk down to your wrongdoing side? Plan three responses to the tyrant that are level, equal, accepting of its wisdom but returning the unused punishment.

For Dyadic and Group Process

1. The biblical study and the exercises for personal reflection are both useful as group exercises. Invite each person to share reflections, learnings, new behaviors he or she planned while working through the material and the experiences.

2. In twos, assist each other in disconnecting self-esteem from social esteem. Internal love values the self that is constant apart from situational stress of success or failure. Feeling good about personhood and feeling glad about performance are two different tasks. Differentiate thinker and thought, behaver and behavior. Give each other clear recognition of worth as a person apart from achieved worth in performance.

3. As a group, experiment with the power of pronouns. Talk for two minutes each in (1) "It" messages that defer responsibility outside the self. "It makes me feel . . ." (2) "We" messages that assume responsibility for all by speaking for the whole group inclusively (and arrogantly I fear). "We all know better, but we do it anyway . . ." (3) "You" messages that are indirect like, "You sometimes

get the feeling," or direct like, "You make me feel inferior when you . . ." (4) "I" messages that speak for the self, from the self. Don't just talk about this, really do it, carefully and reflectively. Note the differences in presence, in genuineness, in congruence, in power as you move from one form to another. As an encore, talk for two minutes only in questions. Then debrief your feelings. Use the chart to try out the various forms of questions which can be used to avoid real contact. Reaffirm your own *I* positions as centered selves that reach out in ways that are not self-centered.

When a man does not acknowledge to himself
who, what, and how he is, he is out of touch with reality,
and he will sicken and die.
And no one can help him without access to the facts.
No man can come to know himself
except as an outcome of disclosing himself to another per-
    son.
When a person has been able to disclose himself utterly to
        another person,
he learns how to increase his contact with his real self,
and he may then be better able to direct his destiny
on the basis of knowledge of his real self.
Sidney Jourard[10]

A man is never so serene
as when he hears himself out,
granting to himself the quieting freedom
to speak fully without fear of self reproach.
Nor is he ever so gravely ill
as when he stops his tongue
with crying out "shame, shame" unto himself.
By stopping up our own ears
against the sounds of our own voices
we achieve not the peace of inner stillness,
but the unnerving disquietude of haunted consciousness.
Wendell Johnson[11]

"I want to know you; I want to be known."

"I'm a little uneasy," Ray said, avoiding eye contact with me. "You've shared too much, too fast for a week-old friendship."

I'm pulling back into myself, momentarily rebuffed. Then I recognize he is telling me about himself as well as criticizing my openness.

It is at the end of our first week of grad school; we've both finished writing 10 hours of field exams. We're exhausted and letting off steam. He tells of leaving his church in Hawaii, I tell of moving across the country from Virginia. Then I share pain. The hurts of leaving a church, a job, a community, the personal and marital tensions come out. Ray nods. He's not only listening, he's saying that he's felt the same pain.

And now his brakes are burning.

I did risk more than he. I didn't wait until he reciprocated when I moved to the personal feeling level.

But he has now taken an even greater risk. By revealing how he feels toward me, here and now, he has dared a deeper level of contact between us than before.

Hearing and being heard is a matter of trusting and risking. Trust and risk go hand in hand. Each

Step by Step, Trust and Risk Are Interdependent

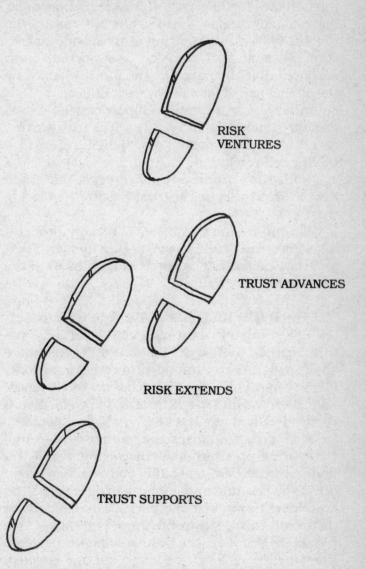

Diagram 12

is dependent upon the other. Any increase in trust is evidenced by taking further risk. Any risk ventured invites further trust. It is as regular as walking, one foot swings ahead as the other bears the weight. With a solid footing of trust, one risks a step forward. As the risk is supported, trust advances. Each is paced by the other, enabled by the other, invited forward by each other.

Initially, risk demands a climate of trust; but to merit trust one must show the self as trustworthy, and the principal means of establishing trust is risking self-revelation. Just as "the chicken is the egg's idea for producing more eggs," to quote Samuel Butler, so risk is trust's way of increasing trust.

Coming to know another is a risky process. Allowing oneself to be known is even greater. Trust and risk are equally required in both sides of the interchange.

"If You Really Understand Me, You'll Love Me"

"Reflecting on last week's conversation, I'm a little scared," Ted says. "I'm afraid I've told more about myself than I intended to reveal to anyone. Maybe you set me up for it by the way you listened, I don't know. But I'm a little afraid to go farther. If you understand me that deeply, will you like me?"

Ted's question poses the two poles of feeling that spring up around self-disclosing: (1) "If you find out what I am truly like, you won't love me." (2) "If you just understood me, you'd love me." The first drives us away from others. The second draws us toward them. Most of us have both poles. One part of the self yearns to be heard and understood. The other hides lest it be found out and rejected. The side which wins in this inner tug-of-war serves as censor to the other. In one person the temptation will be to over-reveal, in another to under-reveal.

The over-revealer may disclose too readily, too fully, too recklessly. At first glance he appears warm, spontaneous, trusting; but a second look shows he may be taking more of your time than appropriate, demanding more of your involvement and support than the relationship warrants. Since he has not learned how to assess what is appropriate to different relationships, the listener has to assume full responsibility for setting limits. In healthy relationships both persons share in defining what a relationship is and in deciding what it will become.

The under-revealer is masked. She reserves control for herself. Cautious and contained, she is concerned about presenting a studied face to the world. She appears disciplined, self-sufficient, or very private. She does not easily reciprocate when another shares personal information.

Transparency is not necessarily a mark of maturity, of good health, or of a sound relationship. What is more important is the balance of respect for privacy and response in intimacy. Each relationship has its own appropriate balance between the two. In one, floating on the surface is indicated. In another, plunging deeply is in order. If the understanding or covenant between two persons calls for growing openness without reservations, then constantly deepening self-disclosure will naturally ensue. Even here, some measure of privacy is important to maintain the integrity of personhood. If the friendship is casual, then superficial sharing may be consistent with the wishes of each. Any move by either to deepen the level of sharing needs some signs of approval or some reciprocity to confirm that the relationship

Concealment Can Sicken
Disclosure Can Heal

The energy poured into concealment impoverishes the person's inner experience.

Loneliness, depression, feelings of falseness, fear of being found out, impulses to hide result.

When one's behavior is viewed as unacceptable, the choice to conceal is costly.

Energy that would have been used in growth of the self is diverted into the growth and maintenance of the mask.

Contact with others is always through the mask; so rigidity, frozen feelings and distance from others inevitably follow.

Diagram 13

can sustain the new depth being ventured.

Developing a sixth sense for measuring the appropriateness of self-disclosure and the depth which the relationship can support is necessary personal equipment for the effective listener.

When Is Openness Healthy?

Both listener and speaker share responsibility for any increase in openness and self-disclosing. The following principles, adapted from the theories and findings of researchers from varied backgrounds, offer 10 guidelines for appropriate self-disclosing for both sides of a conversation.

1. Disclosing is healthful where it is a part of a relationship with a history of continuing trust.

"So you're a marriage counselor?" my seat mate said. "Have I got a question for you!" Twenty minutes later I am still waiting for the question as he pours out the story of his failing marriage. Ventilating to a stranger is of limited use. When I offer a referral, he is not ready to share his name, city, or even state. "I just want to tell somebody my side of the story," he says, and plunges more deeply into disclosing the painful state of affairs—both his affairs and hers.

Emotional streaking is rarely useful. Flashing one's intimate experiences before a stranger only reinforces the problem; it doesn't allow for the solution.

When sharing is not a function of an ongoing relationship with some degree of accountability, it is seldom useful. Instead, participating in a random sharing-of/listening-to intimate parts of another's life only confirms the mistaken idea that it is alright to gossip about a person not present, or that ventilating feelings to an uninvolved third party is helpful.

Depth of Sharing

Speaker	Listener
I will share with increasing depth . . .	I will invite the other to share in increasing depth . . .
1. . . . where it is a part of a relationship with a history of continuing trust.	1. . . . where some measure of trust has been tested by time.
2. . . . where the sharing creates only a reasonable risk, not exciting unmanageable anxiety or requiring more support than is available.	2. . . . where the sharing is a voluntary risk taken by the other, not requiring persuasion, coaxing or reassurances of support.
3. . . . when it fits what has been the character of the relationship previously.	3. . . . where it is a natural progression from our past behavior and will not threaten future openness.
4. . . . as it occurs in two-way interactions of mutual self-disclosure.	4. . . . where there are pauses for equal self-disclosing of our parallel experiences.
5. . . . when it unfolds gradually, bit by bit, not all in one piece so that the risk is based on trust, trust is built on risk.	5. . . . when the self-disclosing is done in small increments so that the speaker is not swept along by the momentum.
6. . . . as each considers the impact the information and the contact are having on the friendship here and now.	6. . . . while reflecting on the effect and/or stopping to explore what impact this revelation is having on our friendship right now.
7. . . . where there are channels to validate or confirm puzzling data.	7. . . . where we are aware of persons, channels, ways to validate what is shared.
8. . . . where neither person feels invaded, absorbed, or rejected by too much closeness; abandoned by threat of distance from the other.	8. . . . where I feel I can stand with the other without absorbing them or being absorbed, without abandoning or inviting rejection.
9. . . . when a crisis of deep misunderstanding or separation may be averted by risking a large amount of new information.	9. . . . when the other is in crisis and needing to ventilate to reduce anxiety, or when a crisis between us requires our being much more open.
10. . . . when there is a recognized social context, friendship understanding, relational covenant or group contract to support the ongoing closeness.	10. . . . when we are connected by a network of friends, a commitment to continuing relationship, a contract for working together, a covenant of caring.

As a listener I want to invite another to share with increasing depth where there is some measure of trust that has been tested by time or where continuing relationships exist. As a speaker I will choose to self-disclose within the relationships which have an ongoing character of integrity.

2. Disclosing is healthful where the sharing creates only a reasonable risk.

"Once I got started, I didn't see a stopping point," Tom says, embarrassment showing. "I'm afraid I've told you more about myself than I wanted to, really, more than I've ever told anyone else in my whole life."

I see in Tom's eyes that he has just been unmasked by his candor. Under the influence of stress he has unveiled parts of himself that he has viewed and still views as private. Can he face me tomorrow, now that I know what he considers unknowable by any other?

I recognized that he was risking a good deal. I could have stopped him and talked about how much trust he was assuming. By discussing this together, trust could have been increased. If he still felt like going public he could have continued.

As a listener I will invite the other to share in increasing depth where that sharing is a voluntary risk, responsibly chosen. If I feel that the person is being swept along by emotion, I want to encourage him or her to share only what is really necessary. I want the sharing to be the other's free choice, not the result of my request, questioning, persuasion or reassurances of support. I will value the other's privacy as I value my own.

3. Disclosing is healthful where it fits what has been the character of the relationship previously.

"I don't understand her at all. Last week she would have nothing to do with me. This week she

Beware of Self-Disclosure!

Be brave . . .
(which means controlled).

Be strong . . .
(which means silent).

Be cool . . .
(which means uninvolved).

Be capable . . .
(which means "on top of things").

Be wise . . .
(which means hidden).

Be admired . . .
(which means hidden).

Self-Disclosure Is Weakness!
Really?

wants to be my friend. A week ago she wouldn't have trusted me with her goldfish, today she was telling me all about the details of her separation from her husband."

Cathy's puzzlement over her co-worker's sudden drive for intimacy begins to make sense a week later when she discovers that June is tiring of *her* and moving on to someone else for her friendship needs. With the pattern of a billiard ball, June bounces from one person to another. Unable to sustain contact she wears out the relationship in a couple of weeks' time, then moves on to another while carrying away any select parts of the last confidante's life story to use for her own ends. Her own needs to ventilate and her demands that the other reciprocate provide immediate and short-lived closeness that does not survive the first tensions of maturing.

Self-disclosure is healthful where there has been a natural, gradual, trustworthy deepening of relationship, so that the new depth ventured is not out of keeping with previous experience and understandings. When a speaker latches on to a listener, like a hungry person coming from famine to feast, there is no basis for estimating the future of the relationship. Thus, risk is best extended only a bit beyond the trust experienced.

As a listener I will invite sharing where it is a natural progression from our past behavior and will check out when it seems too rapid, too disconnected from our previous relationship. Hothouse relationships will be handled with appropriate caution until they have tempered into more hardy, all-weather growth.

4. Disclosing is healthful as it occurs in two-way interactions of mutual self-disclosure.

"I really felt angry at you last night," Sara said.

"I shared a lot of what I had been feeling and going through, and when we quit I realized you hadn't shared anything of yourself. I felt really cheated."

After leading a three-day workshop, I had gone as a houseguest to Sara's home. Sara's husband, Ben, had been a participant, she had been at her job. Now she wanted an equal chance to visit. Exhausted, I simply listened and congratulated myself that I was able to do that when I was so wiped out. Now I realize that I had been less kind than I thought.

To invite another to share deeply and then to not reciprocate leaves the interaction off balance. Or worse, it is an unjust treatment of a friend. If I am too tired to carry on a two-way mutual conversation, the least I can do is admit it early on and offer what energy I have available.

Monologists, verbal road hogs who take up both sides of a conversation by usurping all the time or constantly turning the topic back to the self rather than pursuing common, similar, or shared experiences, are violating the golden rule of hearing as I want to be heard. The listener who supports such monologing is equally responsible for its occurrence.

In the counseling situation it is understood in the contract that one is requesting the privilege of life review with the other's insight and support. Thus, for the moment, normal social interchange is set aside. But as the counseling hour or the series of sessions ends, one of the signs of returning to normal friendship is the resumption of mutual reciprocal interchange with self-disclosure occurring from both sides. As a listener I will invite the other to share and I will claim the pauses for equal, mutual self-sharing to maintain a balance of give-and-take in our communication.

5. Disclosing is healthful when it unfolds gradually, bit by bit, not all in one piece.

"I'm not sure why it took me so long. I'm glad I've gotten to the point of being able to talk about my getting fired with someone who understands, but it took me a while to get here. I think I needed to go step by step until I was ready to tell how deeply it hurt."

"I've had some awfully painful losses too," I respond. "I found I could only share them after I was satisfied that the other person had also felt some of the same feelings."

This excerpt from a conversation is a slice out of many conversations. Relationships grow through interchange, and that happens piece by piece, bit by bit. Friendships are built gradually, except in rare and special circumstances. When one partner deposits a large and substantial piece of information at the other's doorstep, it usually needs to be broken down into subsequent conversation, and the other inserts his or her experiences until a new level of trust has been built.

As a listener I will keep my conversational toe in the door, to give my portion as the dialogue flows along, so that the bridge of shared experience is grounded on both sides, in both our lives. I will interrupt if the other seems swept along by the momentum and give him or her space to reflect by reporting—briefly and with feeling—my own parallel experience.

6. Disclosing is healthful as each considers the impact the information and the contact are having on the friendship here and now.

"Maybe this was more than you could handle today; if so, I'm sorry, but I had to get it off my chest."

The person who excused himself with this line, and then made a quick getaway, had kept feelings and demands in an emotional slush fund for weeks; and then, at an optimum time for him, an impossible time for me, he unloaded A through Z in a setting where two-way dialogue was virtually impossible.

Actually, A through C would have been enough, and adding D through Z was, as the Norwegians say, spreading butter on ham. What were most needed and most sorely missed were a few moments of conversation on what this meant for our relationship here, right now. As the person walked out, I was feeling empty, cut off, sick at the stomach. I wanted to talk.

As a listener I have learned that it is important to reflect frequently on what effect this revelation being shared is having on our friendship right now. If I don't know, it may be more important than the issue we are debating. Try saying, "I need a moment, with all these words being exchanged, to say how important our friendship is to me. I want to get things clear between us so we can feel more comfortable when we are close. What do you want?" Bringing the topic back from there and then to here and now is a bit fearsome; but reconciliation, forgiveness, acceptance can only happen in the here, in the now. It's worth a cautious, gentle risk.

7. Disclosing is healthful where there are channels to validate or confirm puzzling data.

I had this new friend who asked for admiration by telling of fearlessly confronting a New York street gang and walking away unharmed because he was surrounded by the protective wall of faith. He had tears in his eyes as he told the story. The deep feelings touched me, yet I wondered. It was so similar to a movie script I had once seen. Much later, when I discovered a channel to check it out, I found it was not his story at all. Wonderful self-disclosing; too good, but it didn't really bring us together. If we had the tested trust-network of a shared community, then channels for supporting the self-disclosure would have been available. We would have heard each other much more deeply. The truth in the story would have brought us closer. And the desperate cry for attention and respect that was hidden in his dishonest pirating of someone else's experience could have been heard and confronted.

As a listener I want to invite the other to share in a context where we are both aware of persons, channels, ways to validate what is disclosed. Thus, I want to listen to a wife talk about pain in her marriage when the husband is present. I will gently break in as a husband begins to catalogue his gripes about his wife and ask how, when, where we can all three get together to explore this. I will turn the topic when someone is complaining about a person not present to explore how they can get together or whether a third party like me can be of any use.

When the channels are present the data changes a bit, the feelings change a lot, the truth is honored by us all.

8. Disclosing is healthful where neither person feels invaded, absorbed, abandoned or rejected by the other.

Ann interrogates. She asks leading, sometimes trapping questions to find out what she wants. An active listener, when she is deeply involved she becomes a hyperactive listener. I feel invaded, absorbed, controlled.

Joe is a hit-and-run listener. He invites sharing then is finished almost before we've begun. I feel let down, abandoned, stranded in mid-sentence.

These two fears—of being absorbed or of being abandoned—are inside each of us. In most marriages, one partner expresses the one, the other struggles with the opposite. In any intimate relationship either of these—being engulfed or being rejected—will color the feelings that spring up in response to the other.

Disclosing that is heard but not commandeered by the hearer, valued, but not possessively swallowed up, allows the sharer to retain ownership to what is shared and to gather new insight on how to deal with or celebrate what is happening.

Disclosing that is respected, but not with a "that's-your-problem" brush-off, does not leave the speaker with a feeling of being abandoned or ignored.

As a listener I want to invite sharing in a way that guarantees that I will stand with them without absorbing or being absorbed, without abandoning or inviting rejection. I want to be as close as possible without either violating the other's integrity or straining our relationship as two separate, yet caring persons.

9. Disclosing is healthful when a crisis of deep misunderstanding or separation may be averted by risking a large amount of new information. In such a crisis, all of the above steps may be speeded up or temporarily sacrificed in order to open up blocked channels of communication or to restructure a binding relationship.

I thought the working relationship with a particular colleague was open and clear. But I was enough like his father, whom he had never been able to reach, that he carried a lot of mixed feelings hidden behind warm smiles. Then he exploded and turned to walk out. My reassurance that I wanted to hear his beef one more time kept us talking. I am not his father. We were both glad of that. I want to be his brother. We both searched for a way. We shared a year's worth of feelings that would have been discovered bit by bit in less stressful times. We lived a year's worth of normal friendship in a couple hours. We found each other.

When I listen I want to invite the other to disclose whatever may be needed and useful in working through a crisis. If the other needs to ventilate to reduce acute anxiety, or if the puzzlement of our relationship requires our becoming much more open with each other, I want to accept my part, hear the other out, then reach out for new friendship, new growth, new commitment to be present with the other.

10. Disclosing is healthful when there is a recognized social context, friendship understanding, relational covenant or group contract to support the ongoing closeness.

Many people have no intentional relationships. Even their marriages may be contracts of convenience, necessity or coexistence. So self-disclosing is always done—if done at all—at their own risk. In intentional relationships where both parties have clarified their intentions to be friends, brothers or sisters, partners, or fellow group members for a specified period of continuing support, then all sharing is done in shared risk. We are in this business of living deeply, and we are in it together.

The art of covenant making, of striking friendship agreements, of forming groups with clear contracts is the real stuff of which our lives as social beings are made. We are not human alone, since our humanness is a joint substance, a shared quality of interaction as loving persons.

As a listener I know that my invitation to self-disclosing will be healthful when we who share are connected by a network of friends, sustained by a commitment to continuing relationship, or protected by a clear contract for working together toward mutual understanding, or united by a covenant of reciprocal caring.

The Privilege of Privacy

With all these guidelines for healthful self-disclosure, and with so much stress on what can go wrong, perhaps it is wiser to remain a private person. If going public can lead to so many problems, perhaps as Abraham Lincoln observed, "Better to remain silent and be thought a fool than to speak out and remove all doubt."

Privacy, although an important privilege and a necessary discovery in the growth process, is not an end in itself. The realization that one can keep information to oneself is an important step in each person's growth. From the basic trust of early childhood, the toddler develops a beginning sense of autonomy and will. Symbolized by the first uses of the word *no*, it is actualized when the parenting persons respect the child's right to express legitimate preferences and in the firmness to confront and shape the illegitimate *no* into cooperation with other humans.

The right to say no is at the core of identity formation. As one can say a firm no, one can also give a freely chosen yes. The process of maturing in personhood is then worked out through voluntarily self-disclosing larger and larger parts of one's private experience and perspective with chosen others in the creation of community.

"There is a tendency in society to look upon secrecy and privacy as values in themselves," writes Gerard Egan, "even though in the long run they may be self-defeating. In many areas of life the loss imagined to stem from revelation is imaginary. The energy expended in keeping the secret and encoding it—the neurotic may be considered to encode his secrets in his symptoms—is too costly and ill spent. It is much more costly than revelation."[12]

We come to know ourselves through being known by others. To learn to listen in ways that facilitate this is one of the greatest gifts we can give each other.

For Exploration in the Bible

Knowing and being known is a gift we give to each other in risking relationships of trust and love. To explore the deeper meanings of disclosing oneself and discovering another in mutual reverence before God, examine the images and insights in 1 John 1:5-10.

First, examine the definitions of the words John is using as his central images:

light (open, clear, acceptant, revealed, self-disclosed);

darkness (denial, deceit, alienation, hate, hiddenness).

Second, examine descriptions of the relationships John is picturing in his drama:

God is Light. Open, clear, acceptant, revealing light who has self-disclosed in Jesus (vv. 1-3).

We can step out of the darkness and join one another in this open, clear, acceptant circle of self-disclosing people who follow Jesus (v. 7).

But this requires the risk of self-revealing openness, the daring of self-disclosing honesty. It

Privacy and Disclosure

The Privilege of Privacy	VS	The Opportunity to Disclose
Privacy is at the core of identity. Identity is grounded in the right, first, to say "no," and then, a freely chosen "yes."		Disclosing is the process of forming an identity. Identity is nurtured by the give-and-take, the disclosing of self and the discovery of the other.
Privacy is a quality to be discovered then uncovered with some significant other. I truly possess what I can express to another.		Disclosing is a main ingredient for growth. Revelation is good for the person. Admission is good for the psyche. Confession is good for the soul.
Our humanness is not advanced by concealment, by hiding away in separate dens, by safeguarding greater secrecy, by valuing the sanctity of privacy as an end in itself.		Our humanness is set free through more and better communication. The critical concern is not how to keep secrets better, but how to encourage a readiness to communicate.
So, with an awareness of the right to privacy, one matures by relinquishing it.		And with an awareness of the dangers of disclosing, one grows by risking it.

seems so much easier to fake openness, to feign honesty, to fool each other (vv. 6, 8, 10).

So we try to build false communities based on faking, feigning and fooling, but the quality of common-life, community, communion of heart touching heart is lost in the charade.

Meanwhile, God calls us to venture into the light by opening ourselves with each other before the God-who-is-Light. And the more we risk, accept and find ourselves accepted—the more deeply we disclose our own experience the more each truly discovers the other before God. The more fully we see and hear each other the more clearly communication occurs. Community is created, we are walking in the light together.

The end result of such open, disclosing, self-revealing living is the creation of a community of understanding and mutual acceptance. The apostle Paul describes such a community of loving relationship in passages such as Romans 12:1-21; Philippians 2:1-4; Colossians 3:12-17; Ephesians 4:15,16, 25-32. Note how each of these passages, in different words, describes privacy shared in open acceptance, diversity affirmed within a unity, honesty celebrated in mutual respect, a self—disclosed to another and discovered in right relationships with another.

For Personal Growth

The following review will help you evaluate your agreement or disagreement with the points presented in this chapter. Check A-agree or D-disagree. Then compare with the chart on "Depth of Sharing" for speaker and listener.

A   D   1. I think one can share most deeply with a stranger who has no prejudices from the past.

Self-Disclosure Is Basic to Growth

The person
who cannot love
cannot reveal
himself.

The person
who cannot reveal
herself
cannot love.

Self-Disclosure Is the Royal Road to Community

The sharing of the human condition—
its beauty and its deformity,
its joy and its pain,
its wisdom and its folly,
its hope and its despair—
draws us together.

A   D   2. I find people need a nudge to open up, so I share just to break the ice; then I ask good questions.

A   D   3. I feel immediately cautious when someone shares deeply in a way that is uncharacteristic of previous conversations.

A   D   4. I do not interrupt or even feel a need to reciprocate when someone is sharing with me. It would feel like I was competing for the stage.

A   D   5. I think it's good to share a lot about yourself, all at once—like making a plunge in cold water—to get it over with and to get real understanding right from the start.

A   D   6. I sometimes share to get it off my chest whether the other is inviting the whole load or not.

A   D   7. I prefer anonymity, where possible, on things that are really important.

A   D   8. I exercise caution when sharing deeply or when listening so that the other person's autonomy is respected.

A   D   9. I invite persons in crisis to go further in disclosing the sources of their stress than I normally would.

A   D   10. I believe that the most useful and responsible sharing takes place in a context of caring friends and colleagues.

For Dyadic or Group Process

1. Jointly review the chart on "Depth of Sharing"

for both speaker and listener. Each person share memories of effective times of self-disclosing with another person. Compare the observations on the chart with your own experience. Note where your contacts have been exceptions to these rules. Now move to discussion of your own relationship with the people present here and now. Reflect on how far you have gone in self-disclosing, how deeply you have shared, what guidelines you use to decide what is appropriate.

2. Turn to the chart on "Privacy and Disclosure." Reaffirm your own rights to privacy. Restate your own privilege of voluntary choice on how much, how deeply, how frankly, with whom, and at what times you share your experience. Now let the other persons know you also respect their privacy and their right to silence. Reflect on the paradox, "The more voluntariness is respected, the more I am willing to volunteer; the more privacy is prized, the less I insist on keeping private." Do you agree or disagree? How is this evidenced in your relationship?

3. Since self-disclosure is the royal road to community, reflect on how you go about moving toward a bit more intimate sharing each time your relationships deepen, and how you go about drawing back to a less revealing level of communication. As a measuring device, use the following yardstick.

Less intimate Less threatening Gossip	1	2	3	4	5	6	7	More intimacy More threat Encounter
Discussing how Joe felt about Mary, there and then	Discussing how Joe feels about Mary there and now		Discussing how I felt about Mary there and then		Discussing how I feel about Mary now (though she is not here)		Sharing how I felt about you there and then	Sharing how I feel toward you here and now

The miracles of the Church seem to me to rest not so much upon faces or voices or healing power coming suddenly near to us from afar off, but upon our perceptions being made finer, so that for a moment our eyes can see and ears hear what is there about us always.
Willa Cather[13]

He who can no longer listen to his brother will soon be no longer listening to God either, he will be doing nothing but prattle in the presence of God too. Christians have forgotten that the ministry of listening has been committed to them by Him who is Himself the great listener and whose work they should share.
Dietrich Bonhoeffer[14]

Can I let myself enter fully into the world of [another's] feelings and personal meanings and see these as s/he does? Can I step into his/her private world so completely that I lose all desire to evaluate or judge it? Can I enter it so sensitively that I can move about in it freely without trampling on meanings that are precious? Can I sense it so accurately that I can catch not only the meanings of experience which are obvious to him/her, but these meanings which are only implicit, which s/he sees only dimly or as confusion.
Carl R. Rogers[15]

6 ■ Caring

"I will value you as I want to be valued."

"When the word got around that I had cancer," Jan reported, "I soon discovered something surprising about the way I read people. After five or six conversations one day, I realized that I had little doubt about who really cared. Those who 'cared' were those who listened, who really heard me without trying to explain or advise or catalogue their illnesses. It's not hard to tell if you've been cared for. The measuring is done by the listening."

Do you hear Jan? She is scared, confused, angry, and full of feelings that deserve expression. And she is not looking for someone to tell her what to do with her pain or where to go with her problem. She wants presence. Listening is the one sign of caring she recognizes.

"You wouldn't believe the things people say to you when you're going through a separation and divorce," Don said.

"First it's quiet time while they sort out their embarrassment and fears. Then it's old cliché time when they repeat well-worn lines. Then comes inquisition time where they ply you with questions on who's leaving, betraying, rejecting whom. Then it's silence again. Meanwhile, I could sure use a listener who just cares enough to hear my loneliness, puzzlement and sadness."

Do you hear Don? He's not looking for an adviser, a detective, a critic. He wants a friend who cares enough to listen, to hear him where he really needs to be heard.

Listening provides the human connection that is so crucial when one is suffering or experiencing separation or confused about life. It can be the gift of presence that offers a link to humanity when a person feels isolated, alienated, or unwanted by others.

But not all listening is caring.

One can listen for facts, data, detail to use for one's own ends or to quote for other purposes, and so offer no caring at all.

Or one can listen out of sympathy that is energized by pity. To be nourished by one's own pitying is to feed one's pride on the pain of others. To be moved by pity to care is a far different thing. Simple sympathy may not be caring at all.

Or one can listen as another ventilates about a person not present and actually increase the pain and distance between them by implying, through listening, that gossiping about absent others is useful talk. It's not caring at all.

Or one can listen out of apathy or obligation or professional habit or simple niceness, and give no real caring to the other. To care is more than to offer an ear. Habitual hearing may not be caring after all.

Or one can listen inquisitively, with the curiosity of a voyeur peering in at another's private zones. To care is more than to offer wide eyes. The eager ear or eye may not care at all.

Or one can listen "helpfully" as a rescuer with ready first aid, inserting support, understanding, reassurance at each pause. To care is to both give and withhold help. Being chronically helpful may be no help at all.

Yet caring includes elements of each of the above. Accurate attention to what is said, a genuine empathy, a willingness to stand with another when he or she is saying things that are exaggerated through stress, a disinterest that allows objectivity, a willingness to see the other as he or she is, a commitment to be truly helpful as the moment for useful help arrives—all these are ingredients in real care, but they are each clarified and corrected by the central element of caring.

The Essence of Caring

Caring bids another grow.

Caring is an invitation to growth that evokes the best from another. Caring is a motivation that desires what will actualize, complete, mature, fulfill another. Caring is an active willing and working for another's growth, yet it is a sensitive respecting and withdrawing at each possible point so that one does not attempt to do growing for another.

As, in an injury, each cell must reunite with another and no antibiotic can do the growing for the organism, so the caring person can enrich the situation for growth, enhance the possibilities of growth, invite another to grow; but the growth must come from within. No one has ever grown for another. Each is alone in the moment of decision. Growth springs from within.

Caring is coming as close to another as is possible without violating the other's freedom, dignity and self-responsibility. In the closeness, we touch. I hear the sounds of your thrust toward life, your drive toward becoming all you can be, your yearning for relationship, your need for respect as a separate person, your urgency toward growth, maturation and becoming, your responsibility for your self and with the important selves around you. As I hear these I become respectful of your inner compass, reverent before your freedom and responsibility in the moment of deciding, relaxed in trusting your inner wisdom to guide you in finding the next step, painful or joyful though it may be.

Separateness and responsibility for one's own decisions cannot be sacrificed without the loss of one's own identity. The inner estrangement that springs up from living by outer conformity splits the self and drives the inner direction into submission beneath the outer directed controls. No one feels cared for except in the dependency of emergency when another assumes or usurps responsibility for his or her choices. This agent called the *will* will not lightly yield over the opportunity and the obligation of selecting among life's options. Caring *increases* another's alternatives, rather than diminishing them.

In caring, one prizes both the continuity and the difference. I experience myself as a part of you and yet unique. As I listen in solidarity with you I feel the oneness of our humanness. For the moment we may both surpass ourselves and truly touch. When I listen deeply and experience how life appears from your side, separateness is both transcended and reaffirmed.

It is caring that brings goodness to life, creating the *good life,* writes Rollo May with characteristic insightfulness. "Care is a state in which something does *matter.* Care is the opposite of apathy. . . . If we do not care for ourselves, we are hurt, burned, injured. This is the source of identification; we can feel in our bodies the pain of the child or the hurt of the adult. *Life* comes from physical survival; but the *good life* comes from what we care about."[16]

Hearing Is Healing

When hearing is done as an act of caring, it is a healing process. The exact nature of this process will remain forever a mystery, a gift of grace for which we become profoundly grateful as we see it occurring, before which we are rightfully humble as we know we have, in small measure, participated in it.

The dynamics which support and stimulate this process of healing through hearing are millennia old and yet ever new as one receives them from a caring friend. Healing is facilitated as, first, one hears the hurt and accepts it in all its bitterness, numbness or fearfulness; then second, one listens beyond the hurt to hear the voice of the inner healer, invite the renewed hope, resolved will, released pain, restored loving relationship that characterize true healing.

In caring-hearing, the hurt is opened, the festering bitterness of resentful illusions, the burning of angry demands, the numb frozenness of grief, the staleness of depression are allowed to drain. The light is allowed to pour in, sterilizing the infections and stimulating cells of hope and trust to begin new growth.

The hearer-carer hears beyond the hurting the sounds of healing. Sounds the speaker may not recognize until they are heard in the reflections, the quotations, the gentle repetitions of the listener, offering back the whispers of hope heard between the words or said only by the eyes, the hands, the face. Hearing the inner healer's almost silenced cry and inviting it to speak full-voiced is the nature of care. It is no manipulation to nor

In Caring . . .[17]

I experience the other as similar to myself, as an extension of myself, as continuous with myself.

yet

I experience the other as different from myself, as separate from myself, as distinct from myself.

I delight in and invite out growth from within the other, potential from within the other, development in and of the other.

yet

I delight and marvel as it grows in its own right, it discovers, is, fulfills its own self as it becomes who it truly is.

I direct, point the way to growth. I model the directions given. I do not dominate, I stimulate. I am my directions.

yet

I do not impose my direction. I allow the other's direction to guide what I offer or do. In following its growth, I find my own growth.

I may experience the other's well-being as connected, as dependent on my own. I feel needed by it for its growing.

yet

I know that the other's development is autonomous, responsible, on its own. I am not necessary to its growth.

I do not try to help the other grow in order to fulfill and actualize myself. The other is never a means to an end.

yet

As I bid another grow I do fulfill and actualize myself. Seeing another as an end is my means.

As I care, I mature, become, grow. I am fulfilled as a person.
For caring is our calling, our destiny as human beings, our nature as children of God.

so

As I care I invite the other to care. She is fulfilled as a person in caring. He becomes responsive to his need to care. She becomes responsible with self and other. We become respondents in exchanging care.

Caring is direction and devotion.

Caring is letting go and letting grow.

In Caring, I WIll Both . . .

Hear the Hurt   and   *Hear the Healing*

Within each of us there is both

wound	and	healing
despair	and	hope
apathy	and	caring
anger	and	affection
fear	and	confidence
suspicion	and	trust
doubt	and	faith
injury	and	recovery

I want to hear the hurt without seeking to minimize, deny, escape, or too easily alleviate.

and

I want to hear the healing that is already within you, without concluding that healing must come from within me.

guarantee of a cure. But care, not cure, is the listener's task; and where healing results, reverent thanks is given.

Where the stifled whisper of the inner healer is now inaudible, one cares on and on. At such times when one sees the pain repeating itself, cycle on cycle, the caring word becomes, "Come with me, let's find a listener who can hear more deeply and invite healing that neither of us recognizes."

Below Depression

"Wait before you make any conclusions. There's another side to what is being said. Did you hear it? It was there."

Below the words, within the tones, between the lines, comments are often made which throw a new light on what is being verbalized. Hearing deeply is hearing the hidden words that the other may fear to form or feel powerless to express.

Below the depression there is an affirmation. I feel worthless yet I am grieving, for beneath it all lies my awareness of preciousness. Sometimes this sadness is seen only in the eyes or expressed furtively in a single tear. It is the witness of the inner self that "I am worth something in spite of the dead weight of feelings inside this dark mass of despair; I am precious anyway."

The greatest patience, the deepest caution, the tenderest gentleness are required for one to hear these sounds through the heavy cloud-cover of depression. To read them in from one's own awareness of the worth of persons will drive the other's self-awareness even further underground. To reflect them too fast, too brightly, too confidently reveals how little one senses the pain of the depression. But to truly hear those feelings of worth as they emerge, respond to them as they struggle for expression, support them as they take their first steps after being in captivity beneath the imprisoning feelings of helplessness and hopelessness, is to give caring that will call to the inner healer while truly hearing the hurt.

Inside all depression there are judgments that intimidate, imprison, incapacitate the true self and invalidate its deeper feelings of worth. To hear these judgments, and at times to help the other hear them more clearly, can invite the other to begin doubting them and then start disputing them until they have been displaced from the center of the self, back to that part which does useful self-criticism. There the critic can be contained and decontaminated. When one is thus freed, the awareness of inner dignity and worth can speak again and be heard without embarrassment, denial or incapacitating self-criticism. The enduring feelings of self-worth are nurtured, strengthened, given center place.

The most enduring feelings of self-worth come through caring, through caring deeply for others and experiencing their caring for me. Although a sense of worth is "known" innately, sensed spontaneously, affirmed automatically by every person, this awareness of preciousness is shaped by those who give or withhold caring. Caring invites another to claim this preciousness and to allow it to be symbolized in thinking about the self. Uncaring treatment of a child leads him or her to doubt this sense of worth or to divert it into feelings of worthlessness, helplessness and hopelessness. When the inversion is complete, one may even affirm her own sense of worth by denying it. "See how self-effacing I am, how obediently I put myself down? I am acceptable, am I not?"

Caring invites the intuition of the soul to recog-

Hearing Depression

To listen in caring I want to . . .

. . . hear your depression. You have the right to be depressed for as long as you need to grieve about a loss, to feel a particular failure, to accept the hopelessness of false hopes, to realize the helplessness of old strategies that do not work. I want to hear these feelings without seeking to take or talk them away.

. . . hear your judgments. As I hear the "hopeless" judgments you are making about your self and your situation I will invite you to hear them and doubt them. As I hear the "helpless" judgments you are expressing I will also listen for any sign of hope, any hint of self-help and encourage them.

. . . hear your dignity. You are a person of dignity. Your depression is a protest against the loss of that dignity, that sense of value, worth and ability to perform. You are worthful whether feeling high or low, adequate or inadequate, strong or weak.

Inside Depression There Are Judgments

Hopelessness
"My situation is hopeless. I have failed: all is lost, I have fallen: all is discovered, I am ruined: I have lost hope. I am shamed: I must hide. I am hopeless: Nothing will change."

Helplessness
"I am powerless to change. Nothing I attempt
    brings any relief.
Nothing I do
    produces any
    release.
Nothing I try
    reduces the pain.
    I am helpless.
    I am hopeless."

Diagram 14

nize the inner witness of worth, the silent voice that speaks only in feelings—feelings of being loved, being whole, being worthful, belonging.

Listening is the elemental way of embodying such caring. Listening evokes caring from deep within another, it awakens it from within oneself. Listening can become a form of self-renewal. It is a way of becoming more as persons. It is one of the ways we search for ourselves by standing alongside as another is seeking herself. The yearning for self-knowledge is as often satisfied in the hearing of another's discovery of self-understanding as it is in an insight of our own.

In hearing another with reverence, whether depressed or at peace, one can sense the striving for wholeness which is God's own work within us.

Beneath Grief

Beneath the feelings of grief there are other voices to be heard, voices of hopes. Vain hopes and vital hopes.

It is vain to hope that time will stand still, that this moment of loss will not pass and nudge us into an empty future without the one lost. Painful as it is to dwell on the loss, it is less tragic and terrible than the thought of forgetting the one valued so greatly and venturing faithlessly on into life alone.

"When I step into John's woodworking shop in the basement, it is as if he were alive there where his scuff marks show in the shavings, as always before. I catch my breath each time I open the door. No one else has seen it since the last time he worked there. When I miss him most, I go there to be alone with him."

She is caught by hope. A false hope. That hope must die before real hopes can be born.

Caring Enough to Hear and Be Heard   159

Hearing Grief

To listen in caring I want to . . .

. . . hear your grief. I respect your right to live in the past as long as you need to. Grieve deeply. Out of pain felt, savored, honored, released, comes healing.

. . . hear your hopes. I will listen for the hopes, invite them into words, encourage you to express them, assist you in sorting them so false hopes can receive a sad "good-bye" and true hopes can be seen, embraced, trusted.

. . . hear your worth. You have lost persons, experiences or opportunities of great value, worth, importance to you. That is truly, deeply, utterly sad. You are still worthful. Your worth is in no way decreased by your loss. You are worthful not because you have, but as you are.

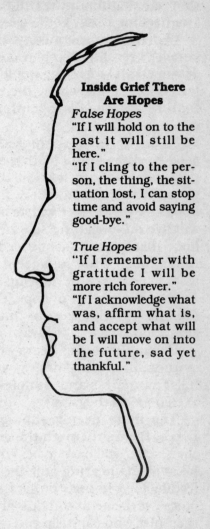

Inside Grief There Are Hopes

False Hopes

"If I will hold on to the past it will still be here."

"If I cling to the person, the thing, the situation lost, I can stop time and avoid saying good-bye."

True Hopes

"If I remember with gratitude I will be more rich forever."

"If I acknowledge what was, affirm what is, and accept what will be I will move on into the future, sad yet thankful."

Diagram 15

It is vain to hope that the pain will subside, the ache will diminish, the emptiness fill without our ever needing to say good-bye.

"When I think about anything I think about us. Lunch? I recall what she would want. Vacation? I dream about where she would want to go. Sleep? I imagine that she will be there when I awake. The sadness and the disappointment are always with me."

He is trapped by the hope that if he does not say good-bye the painful truth may not be true.

Beneath the grief and the false hopes that shroud its surface, there are true hopes. The hopes that the other will be a gift of memory that will live on enriching self and other always. The hope that one can acknowledge what was, gratefully; affirm what is, acceptantly; and welcome what will be, openly. Moving on into the future is sad, yet it is an act of hope. One hopes, not when dreaming of the harvest but when planting the seed. Hope acted is the way to grief released.

Caring-listening hears beneath the grief the sounds of healing hopes, welcomes them into fuller awareness and reinforces any active steps of lived hope as they appear.

The more deeply submerged these healing hopes, the more frozen the grief, the more skilled the listener will need to be. When one is aware that he or she is hearing only the cycles of false hopes feeding false hopes, the gentle support which says "come with me and let us find a skilled listener-therapist who can help you move free" may be the needed gift.

Inside Anger
Anyone who cares will hear a great deal of anger, frequently renamed with more acceptable

words. It is anger still and must be heard as such.

"I'm not angry. I just hurt that she would say-do-act-feel-like that." Hurt is nice, passive anger that places the blame at the other person's doorstep. "I am hurt, thus you are the hurter and I am the hurtee and you are at fault for my pain." When anger is driven undercover in such involuted blaming games, the caring listener gives recognition to the person's right to feel angry without passing judgment on whether he or she is angry rightly. Later when the demands within the anger are clarified, such decisions will be obvious to both.

"I'm not angry. I'm just concerned about the other-the behavior-the relationship-the reputation, et al." Anger is a kind of concern. When the concern is actually a demand, the demand will need clarification, expression or cancellation before release can follow. To hear the demand, invite it to aware verbalization, allows the person to choose how he wishes to respond in aware responsibility.

Tracking down the demands within anger feelings, and differentiating between just and unjust demands, allows the person to negotiate the former and cancel the latter. Unjust demands, when owned in open recognition before another, can be cancelled with the appropriate repentance, release of feeling, often through humor.

"I've been demanding that you do what I want even before I want it. I've called it concern for efficiency. Really it was angry impatience. I will stop playing God. You have your timing. I have mine."

The caring-listener seeks to hear, inside the anger, the inner voice of preciousness denied being preciousness reaffirmed. We are made in such a way that this core need to be valued as

Hearing Anger

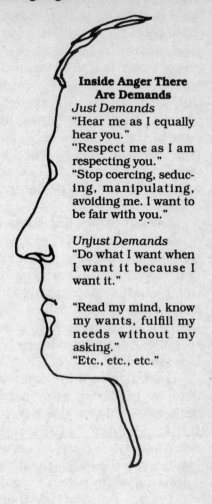

To listen in caring I
want to . . .

. . . hear your anger. I
respect your right to
feel anger. Feelings
are neither good nor
bad, they simply are
a signal that you are
seeing the world
with demands.

. . . hear your
demands. I want to
listen for the
demands, invite
them to surface,
encourage you to
own them, assist
you in deciding how
to express yourself
concerning the just
demands, how to
cancel the unjust
demands, how to let
go of them when
canceled.

. . . hear your pre-
ciousness. You
respond joyfully
when another recog-
nizes your worth as
a person. You react
with anger and hurt
when another does
not see you as pre-
cious and of equal
worth as a person.
You are precious,
worthful, simply
because you are you.

**Inside Anger There
Are Demands**

Just Demands
"Hear me as I equally
hear you."
"Respect me as I am
respecting you."
"Stop coercing, seduc-
ing, manipulating,
avoiding me. I want to
be fair with you."

Unjust Demands
"Do what I want when
I want it because I
want it."

"Read my mind, know
my wants, fulfill my
needs without my
asking."
"Etc., etc., etc."

Diagram 16

worthful is connected to our responses and reactions to those about us. We respond with inner joy and delight when another perceives us as equally worthful. We react with inner pain and anger when we are not so perceived. To truly hear another as the valued person she/he is, is to touch the core of that person and meet a central need of his or her humanness. In listening as caring, this prizing of the other is a deep, often nonverbal invitation to grow in appreciation of self-worth.

Precisely because anger is so commonly condemned as the curse of interpersonal relationships, many people feel a sharp lowering of self-esteem not only as the occasion for anger, as just described, they also feel a decrease in esteem for having been angry. The shame and self-negation gets them both coming and going, with the occasion for anger feelings as its consequence. "I'm getting angry, and I'm angry that I let this get to me, and now this really gets me that I've gotten angry. And after it's over I will really get on myself for having gotten so pushed out of shape over such a little thing." Follow the cycle?

The caring-listener hears inside the anger and the anger about anger, the person's reverence for his or her worth, and invites it into awareness and responsible expression in more constructive relationships. As the inner healer is called out, the pain can subside.

Beyond Resentments

In hearing the hurts of others, one hears many resentments. Phrased quite nicely, they are still the illusory ways of making the self unhappy about what can rarely be changed, and so brooding in self-defeating cycles goes on and on and on.

The caring-listener recognizes the illusions within resentments, since he or she has made peace with some of those in himself or is seeking resolution for others present now in herself. The more fully one has recognized the resentments within himself and come to terms with them, the more freely he can hear the resentments of another without evaluating and advising. The more deeply one has claimed and clarified her resentments and worked through to reality-relationships, the more profoundly she can understand another's resentful illusions without escaping by passing judgments or pressing for simpler solutions.

The illusions within our resentments need to be owned and cancelled in appropriate humility. The godlike pretentions of much resentment are fed by time-illusions. The past can be inverted; we can run it through again and make it right, do it right, set it aright this time. Human clarity begins by recognizing that the past is past and must be seen so. In this present moment I can express anger or regrets, unfinished demands or continuing sadness, requests for change in a relationship or recognition that the attempted cooperation is over. A whole spectrum of possibilities is here, open, now. But the past is not.

The proper response to the past is recognition of then, repentance now, renewal for the future.

The appropriate response to the inevitable is not vain rage against what is unchangeable, but relaxation, reassessment, and redirection.

The caring-listener tunes the ear beyond the hurt of resentment to the healing within the self that reaches toward repented past, realized present and renewed future. To hear any hint of turning from the frozen rage to the thaw of change and

Hearing Resentment

*To listen in caring I want to
. . .*

. . . hear your resentment. You have the right to feel resentment when you perceive a wrong has been done. I want to hear your feelings without evaluations while inviting you to do your own evaluating about what cannot be changed (and so must be accepted) and what can be changed (which must be attempted).

. . . hear your illusions—of grandeur (I can make anything happen), of privilege (I can get even anytime), of deity (I can turn time back), of safety (nothing bad should befall me), of success (no failure should come to me), of revenge (getting even is the only answer). I will check them out to mirror the thoughts for your reflection.

. . . hear your self-image. Beneath the resentments lies the self-image that I want to see, of a valued self that feels devalued. When one has suffered wrongdoing, real or imagined, accidental or intentional, one feels a sharp loss of situational self-esteem. I want to value you by hearing, value you in responding, value you in being with you.

Inside Resentments There Are Illusions . . .

. . . that by holding on to the past with an angry bite I can keep it from being past;

. . . that by making myself unhappy I can make you unhappy too;

. . . that by turning my anger over and over in my mind I can somehow get it right, get even, get back;

. . . that by brooding I can make things better by first making them worse;

. . . that passive anger is more acceptable, useful, powerful, noble than direct open anger.

Diagram 17

to call it to awareness, to fuller reflection, perhaps to action, is a gift of love. In such moments the release of acceptance, the strategizing of how to work toward reconciliation of any fractured friendships, and the nudge toward making forgiveness real can all come from an open ear that hears beyond the resentment, the yearning for reconstruction of severed trust and mutual esteem.

Care Not Cure

In caring, the listener values the respondent regardless of the response, in spite of the performance, without reward of a particular outcome. Not successful cure but sincere care is the goal.

Care trusts the healing process. Cure seeks more. Care is an invitation to growth. Cure is a remedy for illness. Cure is solution, care is resolution.

Care, not cure, is the primary goal of listening.

Care, not cure, is the final goal of life.

There is a place, an important place, for both care and cure, and listening is the primary place to give and receive care.

Caring enough to listen, to listen to the whole person, positive and negative, hurting and healing, is the heart of our human connection one to another. In listening we become truly *with* another. In caring we become truly *for* another. "Being with" and "being for" are the two central elements of loving relationship.

"Don't tell me how much you love me, tell me how much time you have for me" is the bottom line in loving. It is "being with."

"I won't tell you how deeply I love you, I'll show you what I am willing to pass by in the choice to be with you." It is "being for."

In "being with," levels disappear. We no longer reach down or look up to another; we stand with, experiencing each as the same level. Condescension or adulation both are lost from awareness, and mutual trust, co-compassion and admiration develop.

In "being with," I lose the self that is superior, the savior-self, and I discover the self that I truly am as I see and hear the self that you are.

I am I. You are you. We are we. My I-ness is more sharply defined in the act of caring-listening so that I become more truly I, a focal point of open awareness. Your you-ness takes clearer shape as you are cared-for-in-listening; you become more fully you, a firm center of responsible awareness. Our we-ness emerges with cleaner boundaries as caring guides our hearing and being heard. We become more wholly we as our oneness and twoness exist simultaneously without contradiction.

For Exploration in the Bible

The most searching definition of caring-love is given in Paul's first letter to the church at Corinth, chapter 13. I offer it here in covenant form for your reflection, application and integration into caring-listening.

I will give to you	I will seek to listen
love that is patient,	with patience,
love that is kind,	with kindness,
love that is not jealous,	without jealousy,
love that is not possessive,	without possessiveness,
love that is not arrogant,	without arrogance,
love that is not vain.	without vanity.

My love for you
   will not be insensitive or selfish,
   will not be irritable or touchy,
will not be resentful or moody,
   will not be thoughtless or rude.

I will hear you without
   selfishness and insensitivity,
   irritation and touchiness,
resentment and brooding,
   inattention or rudeness.

This love I give
   will not insist on its own way,
   will not keep account of wrongs,
   will not remember past failures.
It will rejoice when good prevails.

I will seek
to see your point of view,
   to spare you my judgment,
   to leave the past behind us,
   to rejoice in your possibilities.

There will be
   no end to its endurance,
   no wavering of its faithfulness,
   no conditions to its trust,
   no hesitance in its hope,
   no limit to its acceptance.

I will be with you
persistently,
   faithfully,
   trustingly,
   hopefully,
   acceptantly.

So my hopes for you
will be constant.
My faithfulness to you
will be sure.
My love for you will be
steadfast.
So faith, hope and love
will endure,
but love will be the
greatest of all.

So hopeful listening
inspires,
faithful listening
encourages,
caring listening accepts.
All three are gifts of love.
Caring-listening is the
greatest of all.

For Personal Growth

In reflection on the learnings from all six chapters, check your experience of the following:

1. I realize that at best, what I see is still an incomplete picture of what might be observed or what really occurred.
2. I realize that what another reports about any situation or person is a condensed version of what might be said or is actually available.
3. I realize that my interests and feelings filter what I see, hear, think, feel, say and do. I recognize that this is true for others as well.
4. I use language in such a way as to specify the main parts of a message so that the intent and the impact are as nearly the same as is possible.
5. When I speak I take into account the probability that some of my words will be misinterpreted; I seek both to be understood and to not be misunderstood.
6. I am alert to nonverbal signs of misunderstanding and I adjust to such silent feedback by restating and improving.
7. I avoid "allness" by quantifying and qualifying; I move from the abstract to the concrete,

from there and then to here and now when-
ever possible.

8. I use words showing degrees of difference
   when possible rather than two-value words,
   speaking of more or less rather than either-or.

9. I seek to suspend judgment and to understand
   what a speaker means in terms of her frame of
   reference before I react to her statement.

10. I am aware of whether I am stating observa-
    tions, interpretive inferences, value judg-
    ments, or personal feelings and call the opin-
    ion, feeling, thought or judgment what it
    actually is.

For Dyadic or Group Process

1. Each person write the definition of "caring"
   that you have used in your thinking to date (or
   a series of definitions as you note a progressive
   evolution of understandings). Now mix the
   sheets in a hat, each draw one and in turn read
   the definitions and let the others identify the
   writer. (How a person defines caring and how
   he or she goes about caring is one of the central
   and unmistakable characteristics of that personality. Note how quickly, clearly, easily the
   recognition process occurs.) Now compare your
   answers with the chart entitled "In Caring. . . ." Note and explore agreements and disagreements.

2. Each person choose a chart which maps a
   major emotion—depression, grief, anger,
   resentment—for which you have a strong affin-
   ity or which you have deeply experienced. In
   silence compare your experience with the
   description of the dynamics of that particular
   emotion as it is outlined inside the profile of a
   face. Make notes on how you experienced the
   respective demands, hopes, judgments or illu-

sions in these moments of deep feelings. When the meditation time is past, each person share agreements, disagreements, discoveries or puzzlement. Invite the others to clarify by sharing their own experience of this same emotion. (Do not question, analyze, or try to problem-solve for the other person. Simply share the gift of self-disclosure and the real hearing of the other's feeling.) Honor each person's right to feel what he or she feels, experience life as he or she experiences it.

3. On Caring. Return to the chart "In Caring. . . . Reflect on the ways in which you have experienced giving and receiving care by finishing the following lines.
   "I feel cared for when . . ."
   "I care most deeply by . . ."
   "I want to grow in caring by learning to . . ."
   "I want to be more caring by refusing to . . ."
   "When I need more caring I will . . ."
   "When you are longing for caring, please . . ."
   Now share the feelings, learnings, new behaviors that have been stimulated by working through these experiences together.

4. Give each other gifts of (1) appreciation: "I appreciate your . . ."; (2) admiration: "I admire the way you . . ."; and (3) stimulation: "I heard you say that you want to. . . . How can I nudge, prompt or celebrate it with you in the future?" Listen to the caring given. Receive it. This is a gift in return.

5. Pray together: "O God, may the eyes within my eyes be clear, the ears within my ears be open, the hearing beneath all hearing be truly present.

                                                    Amen."

■ Notes

1. Paul Tournier, *To Understand Each Other* (Atlanta: John Knox Press, 1967), pp. 29,30.

2. Paul W. Keller and Charles T. Brown, *From Monologue to Dialogue* (Englewood Cliffs, NJ: Prentice Hall, 1973), p. 6.

3. Abraham Schmitt, *The Art of Listening with Love* (Waco, TX: Word, Inc., 1977), p. 12.

4. Earl Koile, *Listening As a Way of Becoming* (Waco, TX: Word, Inc., 1977), p. 21.

5. Reuel Howe, *Herein Is Love* (Valley Forge, PA: Judson Press, 1961), p. 30.

6. Keller, Brown, *From Monologue*, p. 199.

7. Milton Mayeroff, *On Caring* (New York: Harper and Row Publishers, Inc., 1971), p. 37.

8. Tournier, *To Understand Each Other*, p. 16.

9. Hugh Prather, *Notes to Myself* (Moab, UT: Real People Press, 1970).

10. Sidney Jourard, *The Transparent Self* (New York: Van Nostrand Reinhold Co., 1971), p. 5.

11. Wendell Johnson, *Your Most Enchanted Listener* (San Francisco: International Society for General Semantics, 1972), p. 21.

12. Gerald Egan, *Encounter* (Belmont: Brooks-Cole, 1970), p. 202ff.

13. Willa Cather, *Death Comes for the Archbishop* (New York: Alfred A. Knopf, Inc., 1927), p. 50.

14. Dietrich Bonhoeffer, *Life Together* (New York: Harper and Row Publishers, Inc., 1976), pp. 98,99.

15. Carl R. Rogers, *On Becoming a Person* (Boston: Houghton Mifflin, 1961), p. 53.

16. Rollo May, *Love and Will* (New York: Dell Publishing Co. Inc., 1969), p. 286.

17. Adapted from concepts in Milton Mayeroff, *On Caring*.

■ Acknowledgements

The following writers and sources have shaped or contributed to the concepts in the following:

Chapter 1 draws from Erik Erikson's description of the human life cycle in his book *Identity: Youth and Crisis;* Robert Butler's reflections in his various writings on *Life Review Therapy* guide my comments on listening and aging.

Chapter 2, the ten commandments for listening, are adapted from Jud Morris, *The Art of Listening.*

Chapter 3, the levels of interpersonal address have been articulated by many people, although none exactly as here presented. The closest is the work of Sir Geoffrey Vickers of M.I.T.

Chapter 4 utilizes the understandings of Murray Bowen on taking an I-position as a way of differentiating selfhood, *Family Therapy in Clinical Practice.*

Special appreciation to *The Festival Quarterly,* Lancaster, PA, in which portions of this chapter first appeared in brief articles.

Chapter 5 is enriched by the work of Sidney Jourard, *The Transparent Self,* and Joseph Luft, *Of Human Interaction.*

Chapter 6 is shaped by the best integrative work

on caring as a stance toward life, Milton Mayeroff, *On Caring* and Eric Fromm, *The Art of Loving.*

Bibliography

Bonhoeffer, Dietrich. *Life Together.* New York: Harper and Row Publishers, Inc., 1976.

Bowen, Murray. *Family Therapy in Clinical Practice.* New York: Jason Aronson, Inc., 1978.

Butler, Robert. *Life Review The, Psychiatry,* Vol. 26, 1963.

Cather, Willa. *Death Comes for the Archbishop.* New York: Alfred A. Knopf, Inc., 1927.

Erikson, Erik H. *Identity: Youth and Crisis.* New York: W.W. Norton and Company, Inc., 1968.

Fromm, Eric. *The Art of Loving.* New York: Harper and Row Publishers, Inc., 1974.

———— *Love and Will.*

Howe, Reuel L. *Herein Is Love.* Valley Forge, PA: Judson Press, 1961.

Johnson, Wendell. *Your Most Enchanted Listener.* San Francisco: International Society for General Semantics, 1972.

Jourard, Sidney M. *The Transparent Self.* New York: Van Nostrand Reinhold Co., 1971.

Keller, Paul W. and Brown, Charles T. *From Monologue to Dialogue.* Englewood Cliffs: Prentice Hall, 1973.

Koile, Earl. *Listening As a Way of Becoming.* Waco, TX: Word, Inc., 1977.

Luft, Joseph. *Of Human Interaction.* Palo Alto, CA: Mayfield Publishing Co., 1969.

May, Rollo. *Love and Will.* New York: Dell Publishing Co. Inc., 1969.

Mayeroff, Milton. *On Caring.* New York: Harper and Row Publishers, Inc., 1971.

Morris, Jud. *The Art of Listening.* Boston: Industrial Education Institute, 1968.

Outka, Gene. *Agape.* New Haven: Yale University Press, 1973.

Prather, Hugh. *Notes to Myself.* Moab, Utah: Real People Press, 1970.

Rogers, Carl R. *On Becoming a Person.* Boston: Houghton Mifflin, 1961.

Schmitt, Abraham. *The Art of Listening with Love.* Waco, TX: Word, Inc., 1977.

Tournier, Paul. *To Understand Each Other.* Atlanta, GA: John Knox Press, 1967.

Other Regal Books to help you build better relationships: